A JOURNEY TO INNER HEALING

A
JOURNEY
TO
INNER
HEALING

*Understanding the
Mind–Body–Spirit
Connection*

Louis P. Bauer, Ph.D.

*Audubon Publishers
Slidell, Louisiana*

For information, contact the publisher:

Audubon Publishers

1234 Audubon Street

Slidell, LA 70460

Grateful acknowledgement is made to Bernie Siegel for permission to quote from *Peace, Love and Healing* by Bernie Siegel, M.D. © 1989, and *Love, Medicine and Miracles* by Bernie Siegel, M.D. © 1986; and to Larry Dossey for permission to quote from *Reinventing Medicine* by Larry Dossey, M.D. © 1999; and to Arlin Verman and Universal Designers, 855 West New York Ave., De Land, Florida, for permission to include photo in Chapter 9, "*Being in God's flock ...*"

First Edition

Printed by:

Eerdmans Printing Company

Grand Rapids, Michigan

ISBN 0-9720622-9-7

Library of Congress Control Number: 2002092467

Preface

How would you like to discover a treasure trove of unlimited wealth, a treasure so vast it would forever change the way you live? You won't find it at the end of the rainbow. It's not resting upon the ocean floor. It's buried only as deep as *you* choose to hide it.

It's the treasure of the mind, body and spirit, and once you discover it and unlock its secrets, it will give you power—the power to change your life, the power to control the situations in your life instead of being controlled by them, the power to overcome problems instead of becoming overwhelmed.

This power was a God-given gift to each of us at the time of our birth, but most of the time it remains unrealized.

My purpose in writing this book is to help you realize the awesome importance of harmony between the mind, body and spirit, and to share with you the tools and techniques needed to achieve it. Once you achieve this harmony you will live a happier, healthier, more peaceful and more productive life than ever before.

I know firsthand the devastating consequences that can take place when this harmony is lacking, because its absence was the source of a severe depression that almost destroyed me. That is, until I experienced a miraculous healing, which I share with you in Chapter 1. It had a profound effect on me that totally altered the course of my life and led me to the place I am today.

As a Christian clinical hypnotherapist, I incorporate a person's own spirituality in the healing process and I've seen many miraculous things take place. They have no logical or medical explanation, but they happen.

Through my experiences with clients I realized that there are many people who, each day, deal with the same anger, hurt, guilt and negative feelings that I did, never seeing the big picture and not knowing how to make a change for the better. This realization was the major motivator for writing this book.

Throughout the book I refer to biblical scriptures and the teachings of Jesus. If you don't believe in Jesus, don't discount the stories, just think of him as a wise teacher.

Some people may not agree with everything in this book, and that's okay. Just take what's yours and leave the rest. It may be surprising to you that within a week, a month, a year or even more, you will pick up this book again and, lo and behold, find that what you left in the past are the words of wisdom you need now.

Acknowledgements

When I sit back and ponder life's journey, I realize that there are many people along the way who have not only made this book possible but also helped me turn my dreams into reality.

I would like to thank: first and foremost, God, for this glorious adventure. He's given me wings to fly over the rough spots and always led me where I needed to be (even though sometimes I was pulling in the opposite direction).

My wife, Deana, for her immense love, constant support, her infectious laughter and her limitless patience (I know, because I've tested it!). You are my cherished traveling companion and truly the wind beneath my wings.

My older son, Louie, who was always there for me. Your loving and spiritual family has been a great source of joy in my life.

My second-born son, Danny, whose time upon this earth was all too brief. You've always been in my heart.

My younger son, John, who always showered me with love and who, at age twelve, gave me the book *Jonathan Livingston Seagull* for Christmas. Inside the cover he had written these encouraging words, which still remain planted in my heart: *"Dad, Remember always go after your dreams and explore your curiosities, for it is through persistence that you succeed."*

My one and only daughter, Cathy, who was the one person responsible for helping to make this book a reality. If it were not for her, this book would have gone with me to my grave. She gave so much of her time and of herself—going through all the data, information and research, and doing endless hours of typing—to make this book possible. I would also like to thank her children, for the unselfish way they did without her so she could help me fulfill my dream, and my son-in-law, Bob White, for his constant support and friendship.

My dear friends who have not only shared this wonderful journey but also shared their love, support and encouragement in making this book possible—Lilly Martin, Paul Durbin, Pat Richard, Sheila Smith, Avis and Marvin Burnette, Father John Izral, Father Robert DeGrandis, Ruth and Arthur Serpas, and Robert and Cindy Cornibe.

And last but certainly not least, I want to thank all of my clients, especially those who gave me permission to use their testimonies and even their real names. You've helped me grow in knowledge, been a constant reminder of the power of God and become my treasured friends.

This book is dedicated to you.

I am also deeply grateful to the following people, whose knowledge and skills have helped make this book possible—a special thank-you to my son Louis Bauer for his early-morning treks and photography skills that captured the awesome cover photo; to my daughter, Cathy White, who designed the cover layout; to Virginia Iorio for her astounding copyediting skills; to Jay Van Dyke of Eerdmans Printing Company for his sage advice and boundless patience; and to Mike Sanders of Visions Photography in Slidell, Louisiana, for his infinite knowledge and for supplying the interior photos.

Preliminary Statement

I am not a medical doctor and this book is in no way intended to take the place of medical treatment. It is intended merely to motivate one to incorporate all aspects available (body, mind and spirit) in the healing process.

Louis Bauer's passion for his work and compassion for people screams through these pages. He is disarmingly honest and down to earth. The Christian community need not fear clinical hypnotherapy, especially when guided by a professional who embraces Christian values, since Jesus often used trance induction through storytelling to open his audience to a life-changing truth. I know this man, his story and methodology. He has a heart for God and simply wants to share what he has learned through his own journey. He reminds me of the blind man in the temple who, when frustrated by constant questioning from the Pharisees, exclaimed: *"All I know is I once was blind but now I see!"*

Louis, thanks for making me a part of your experience.

—G. Reid Doster, DMin., L.P.C.
Licensed Professional Counselor

Dr. Bauer has combined his professional training with that of a gifted wordsmith and, most importantly, his understanding of life as a true Christian gentleman, in producing this guide to living. You will find yourself returning to it long after your first healing trip through its chapters.

—Philip White
Journalist and free-lance writer

Contents

Chapter 1

The Journey Begins

I want you to imagine yourself taking a trip—a journey to an exciting and exotic place that you've always dreamed about. How would you get there? Where would you begin? You wouldn't just hop in your car and begin driving without directions, and you certainly wouldn't just show up at the airport and get on a plane without knowing where you were headed. You would need a road map, a guide to your dream destination. You would want to know the easiest, fastest and safest way to get there. You would learn about the place you are going to, so you wouldn't be confused about the best spots to visit. You would carry your map with you and you would refer to it from time to time, so you wouldn't take a wrong turn or get off at a wrong exit.

Life is the greatest journey of all, yet many people wander aimlessly down the road. They may know what they want their destination to be, but they have no road map to guide them. They have no knowledge of how to reach their destination, so they get sidetracked. They become confused and overwhelmed.

It reminds me of the story of a farmer and his little dog. One day the farmer loaded the harvest into his wagon and headed to market in the city. As the horse and wagon clip-clopped down the road, the little dog ran right alongside of him. A little way down the road, the dog picked up the scent of a rabbit and off into the woods he went. The old farmer continued down the road, taking his time, and after a few minutes the dog returned. He was out of breath from his adventure but kept right on following the wagon. A little farther down the road, the dog picked up another scent and raced off into the woods. This time he was gone even longer, and when he returned he was bleeding. He had cuts on his ears, burrs in his coat and was so out of breath he could hardly keep up with the wagon. He was totally exhausted. They traveled on a bit farther, and soon the dog took off again, after some elusive scent.

The farmer reached the town and began to unload his wagon. The storekeeper came out and asked the farmer, "Where is your little dog?" Just then they looked up the road and saw the little dog limping toward them. He was all cut up and could barely make it. He was so thirsty that there was foam coming out of his mouth. The storekeeper gasped, "My goodness, you all must have had a terrible time getting here today!" "No," said the old farmer, "the journey was easy. It was all the sidetracks he took that were so rough on him."

Many times we, like the little dog, journey through life without a clear vision of our destination. Without a definite plan, we lose our focus on the goal we want to achieve and we get lost.

Achieving anything in life requires a definite plan. That is my purpose in writing this book. I want to give you a road map—a guide to help you achieve your goals, reach your destination and enjoy the journey. I want to share with you the knowledge you will need to help you avoid getting side-tracked and taking the wrong turns that will lead you far away from your goals.

Before you begin, it is important to have a clear-cut picture of what it is you are looking for. Ask yourself, what do I want to achieve? What do I want out of life at this moment? It is important that you don't look too far down the road; any great journey begins with but a single step. Think about now. What do you want? Do you want to be happier? healthier? more peaceful? Do you want to be more productive? Do you want to gain knowledge? Would you like more confidence and self-esteem? Would you like to be more in control of situations and circumstances?

This book will give you the tools, the information, the knowledge, motivation and determination needed to help you achieve the goals you set for yourself. It will inspire you, in a profound way, to become the person you want to be. The dictionary defines inspiration as "a divine influence on a person; the act or power of moving the intellect or emotions." When you are divinely inspired, you have more than motivation. You have *power*!

It is also important for you to understand that there is a connection between the mind, body and spirit that is vital to your well-being. Chaplain Paul Durbin, a dear friend and the author of the book *Kissing Frogs: The Practical Uses of Hypnotherapy*, refers to it as the "Human Trinity" of body, mind and spirit. He states, "These three aspects of our being are so different and yet so integrated that one part of the Human Trinity cannot be affected without having some effect on the other two."

This is not just a concept I understand, but one I totally believe in because I experienced firsthand the dangerous results that can come when this trinity is out of balance.

Think of it this way. All of us are familiar with paper dolls—flat, one-dimensional images with no substance, unable to stand on their own. When this trinity of mind, body and spirit is out of balance, there is a lack of harmony within our lives. We become very much like a paper doll: one-dimensional. Life begins to feel empty, lacking in some way. When problems arise, we can't see our way around them because we're viewing them from only one perception, whether that perception is right or wrong. We can't see the forest because of the trees. We can't seem to overcome our problems, so they overcome us. We become negative, and negativity buries the spirit. Just remember, the mind may control the body, but we control the mind. When we fill our mind with positive thoughts, it has a positive effect on the body. When we let go of negative emotions such as anger, hatred, guilt and bitterness, we release the spirit and our lives become full of joy and peace. We become whole again: three-dimensional. We are no longer overcome by problems because we have new perceptions and we can see our way clearly around them.

I feel it necessary to share with you my journey of self-discovery so that you understand the extreme importance of harmony within the mind, body and spirit. This is not just a subject that I studied, but also a life lesson that I learned through experience. In 1987, at age fifty-three, I was fairly happy with my life. I had a great wife and three children, two of whom were grown with families of their own and one who was soon to enter high school. For twenty-five years, I had a career in sales. I felt secure in my job and truly enjoyed it.

4

My sales territory consisted of all of Louisiana and part of Mississippi. Although it was a large territory and required a lot of time and energy, I didn't mind. Over the years, I had built a great relationship with my customers so that whenever I called on them it was like visiting old friends. They trusted me and knew that when they bought something from me, I came with it. They knew I would be there to service them or help in any way possible. It was a pleasure getting up and facing the world every morning because I felt good about the job I did. I was also looking forward to retirement in a few years and finally spending that special time with my wife, doing the things we always dreamed of. Life seemed good.

Then, slowly, the threads that held my world together began to unravel. My boss informed me that there would be a reorganization of employees. The large, profitable sales territory that I had built up since I started with the company was going to be split up with a younger employee. They reduced my sales territory drastically, which meant basically starting from scratch. As a good portion of my salary came from commissions, I was horrified. This not only meant quite a bit less money coming in, but I was back to knocking on doors and cold-calling on new clients. I felt angry, hurt and betrayed. Here I was, close to retiring, at a point in my life where I felt I would be able to reap the rewards of all my hard work, and it was being taken away from me. To make matters worse, I found out that a co-worker was spreading false rumors about my job performance. I felt I didn't deserve all of this, yet it was happening to me. I began to take it personally and felt that they were trying to make it hard for me. I was also worried that any day I might be laid off because of the reorganization. I grudgingly accepted the new task, but each day I became more resentful and bitter. With the resentment came anger—anger with my boss, the company and even with my co-workers. Soon the anger began to reach out even further, even to some of my clients. Then there came a point when that anger turned into hatred. All my life, I tried to do the right thing. I respected other people and tried to help them whenever they needed it, and this is the treatment I got in return! What I didn't realize then is that anger and hatred have a snowball effect. They keep growing and extending to all areas of your life until finally they take over completely. These feelings consumed me, and soon every little molehill in my life became an insurmountable mountain.

I became less tolerant with people. If a car pulled out in front of me in traffic, I just wanted to hit it. I even considered buying an old truck and putting an old railroad bumper on it so that if someone pulled out in front of me, I could really let them have it. I also had a neighbor who at that time decided to start collecting junk, which was fine until he started using my fence to lean it all on. Trying to talk to him was useless and it ended up in a shouting match, at which point I told him exactly what I thought of him. I tried to forget about it but I couldn't. Every time I came home my eyes went straight to the fence to see what new junk he had collected, and my anger would start all over again. But each time my anger would grow greater because I felt I didn't deserve to be treated that way. I would never treat someone else that way. I had always respected other people's property, but no one respected mine. You see, the snowball just kept growing.

I tried to go on vacation, just to get away from it all, but it followed me. I went scuba diving, but even twenty feet under the water, I was still reliving all of the anger I had experienced. I couldn't escape from it. It was totally possessing me!

My life continued on this way for over a year until something strange happened. I was calling on a client one morning and as I pulled up in front of his office, I began to cry. I didn't know why I was crying, so I left. I stopped at a restaurant to try to regain my composure. I went to the rest room and washed my face. When I came out I ordered a cup of coffee, and after sitting there for a while I began to feel better. I decided to go back to my client's office, but as soon as I drove up I began to cry again. I couldn't understand what was happening and I couldn't control it. I just had to leave. I cried the entire thirty miles back home, uncontrollably, like a child with a broken heart. I kept looking out of the window to see if anyone was looking at me. I felt foolish but I couldn't stop. When I got home, my wife asked, "What's wrong?" "I don't know," I told her, "I just feel depressed." She suggested that I go to bed and get some rest, so I did.

From then on, it was downhill. I spent about three weeks in that bedroom. I didn't want to come out. All I wanted to do was close the blinds and just sleep.

It seemed as if there was a fast-forward tape constantly playing in my mind, and I couldn't slow it down. I kept thinking, "What if I lose my job? What if I say something about how I feel and they fire me? After all these years, what am I going to do? I don't have anything to fall back on or anywhere else to go. What if my neighbor stacks more junk on the fence? It's already beginning to bow under the weight. What if he comes into my yard and wants to start trouble?" My mind was filled with what-ifs and I kept thinking how unfair it all was. It just wasn't right. These thoughts and all of the anger and hurt kept playing over and over in my mind until it overwhelmed me. The only time I got any relief from these thoughts was when I was asleep. I didn't have to deal with anything or anybody. Sleep was a form of escape, so that's all I wanted to do. Things had gotten so bad that I even considered taking my own life because I felt I just couldn't handle it anymore.

My family tried to help me and comfort me, but all I wanted was to be left alone. I felt as if I was the only one in the world who felt that way. How could I explain to anyone the strength of my anger and resentment? I was sure no one would understand.

My older son, Louie, would come and ask me to take a walk with him. I wanted to, but I didn't want to leave the security of my bedroom. Friends and family would try to help by telling me that I shouldn't feel that way, that I had a good job, a great family. I knew these things already, but it didn't matter. It only made me feel worse. I just couldn't change the way I felt.

One afternoon, my wife, Deana, came into the bedroom and said, "Honey, I've fixed you something to eat. Why don't you come in the kitchen and eat and maybe we could talk a little?" I told her, "Look, why don't you just get out of here? Just leave me alone, will you?" She closed the door and went out into the hallway. I could hear her begin to cry, pitifully. I got up, filled with anger, and went out there. "What the hell are *you* crying for?" I yelled. I felt like I was the one who was hurting, so what reason did she have to cry? She just looked up at me and said, "I love you so much and I just don't know what to do to help you." I knew that there was something wrong with me, but I didn't know what it was. Because I had no control over my feelings, I was frightened. I thought I was losing my mind. When my wife said that to me, it struck something inside of me and I told her, "I need to get some help. This isn't me. I just don't know what's wrong with me."

Deana took me to a psychiatric hospital so that I could check in and maybe get the help I needed, but I wasn't sure this was the right step. I went inside and looked around. Some people were sitting there, staring off into space, some were talking to themselves, some were huddled in the corners, and I thought, "Wait a minute, I don't belong here!" I turned to her and said, "Look, I think I'm just going to leave. I don't think this place is for me. I don't belong here!" She said, "Well, if you want to leave, get your suitcase and we'll go." But I realized I needed some kind of help, so I said, "No, I'll stay." But when she left and walked out that door, I think that was one of the most frightening moments of my life!

The doctors put me through a whole series of tests, and the diagnosis was that I had a chemical imbalance that was causing the depression. It was such a relief to find out that there was something physically wrong with me that caused me to feel the way I did. I was started on some medications, but they caused some bad side effects. The doctors then decided to put me on a different medication, which they said was much slower acting. It would take about thirty days to get into my system well enough to have any effect. It would probably be a number of months before I would even wake up in the morning and not feel severely depressed. I was informed that I would have to remain on the medication for the rest of my life or else I would go right back into that severe depression.

During my first two weeks there, I was not allowed to be anywhere alone. I had told them how depressed I had been and that I had even considered taking my own life, so they felt that they really needed to watch me. I wasn't allowed to go outside in the courtyard alone, and anytime I went anywhere, someone was with me. I was in the hospital for about two and a half weeks when they gave me a two-hour pass. Deana came to pick me up and said, "Why don't we go home? I've fixed a dinner for you, and the kids are there. I thought that you might like to see them." But I said no. I knew I couldn't go home then because the minute I turned the corner and saw the neighbor's yard, it would just be too much. I couldn't go back to that bedroom where I had stayed for so long feeling depressed and thinking of ways to end my life. I just couldn't go back into that environment. I said, "Let's just stay here."

I was beginning to feel somewhat protected in the environment of the hospital. I didn't have to worry about anybody because I wasn't allowed visitors. But I also knew that it wasn't going to last. I knew I was using up my savings, and I was probably going to lose my job and my home, and I didn't know how long my family would be able to put up with me. To say I was afraid would be an extreme understatement.

We sat together for a little while and then I asked her to take me to the church. Let me tell you, church was the *last* place I wanted to go. I couldn't believe those words came out of my mouth. You see, I resented God—big-time. My thoughts were, "If you're such a good God, then why is all this happening to me? I've always tried to do the right thing, treat other people with respect. I don't deserve all the things that have happened to me. If you were truly a *loving* God, you wouldn't let these bad things happen." But that night, we went to church anyway. The church was closed, but the chapel was still open because of perpetual adoration.

It was 8 o'clock and we were the only ones in the chapel, which seemed strange because there was always someone in the chapel.

We knelt down in the front pew and I tried to pray. I tried to say the Lord's Prayer and even all the prayers I had learned as a child, but I couldn't. I just couldn't pray. I felt like such a hypocrite because I didn't want to be there. I couldn't let go of all the hurt and anger I was feeling. I would have left, except when I looked over at Deana, she was kneeling down praying intensely. I didn't want to disturb her, so I sat down in the pew and just stared at the altar, on which sat the monstrance that held the Eucharist. As I stared, it was as though the fast-forward tape, filled with all these negative thoughts that had been playing over and over in my mind, began to slow down. I thought, "Well, I'll just go back to work and do the best I can. And if they fire me, well, they'll just fire me. I'll find something else. But what am I going to do? I don't know anything else. But, it's okay, I'll find something else." And then I began to think of other things I could do. I closed my eyes and I thought, "I'm going to say a prayer for my boss, even though he did that to me." But when I thought that, it was as if someone reached down into my stomach and twisted my intestines. "You fool, you're going to forgive him after all the rotten things he did to you?" But I thought anyway, "I'm still going to say a prayer for him and his wife."

And as I sat there, with my eyes closed, I began placing these people for whom I was praying in a clockwise circle in my mind. I thought, "I'm going to say a prayer for my neighbor and his wife." And again, I experienced that physical feeling of pain. It was as if my stomach was knotting up inside of me. I was literally fighting an internal battle. But I

11

thought, "I'm still going to pray for them. And I'm going to say a prayer for that co-worker who'd been spreading lies about me. Even though some people believed those lies and it hurt me, I'm going to pray for him. And I'm going to pray for this person and for that person." And as I continued putting these people within that circle in my mind, there was a rush of more and more people that I needed to pray for. But through all of this, I still had that terrible twisted feeling in the pit of my stomach. I thought, "It's so hard. I don't know if I can let go of this." Suddenly, in the center of the circle in my mind, appeared a dark circle, and out of the darkness came a thought, a thought so powerful and strong, I knew it didn't come from me. It said, "*Do it for Me.*"

At that instant, all of the anger, hatred, resentment, bitterness, jealousy, revenge and depression were gone. Totally gone! Never, in my entire life, had I experienced the peace that I felt that night. I started crying and went outside the church. Deana followed me and asked what happened. I told her about my experience and she asked me, "Louie, what did you do?" "I didn't do anything. I don't understand it. It's like it was all taken away—totally taken away. I just can't explain how I feel now. None of it is there. I'm not depressed. I feel absolutely wonderful!"

I went back to the hospital and asked the nurse, "What's the chance of my going home tomorrow? I'm okay," and I told her what happened. She told me that I would have to speak to the psychiatrist about that. The next day the psychiatrist came in and I said, "Look, Doc, I want to get out of here because I'm okay now," and I proceeded to tell him what happened. Needless to say, I think he thought that I'd totally lost it now. He said, "I just can't let you go like that. When you signed in here, you gave us the right to hold you, even against your will, for at least seventy-two hours, until we can be sure you're not a danger to yourself or others. We would have to run more tests on you before we could even consider letting you go." "Doc," I said, "do what you have to do, but I want out of here because there's nothing wrong with me." They ran the tests and miraculously the chemicals were all back in balance. Since that night in the chapel, I've never taken any medications for depression and I've never again experienced any symptoms of the illness.

From that moment on, I began a new journey. I knew then that I wanted to help people. I didn't know exactly how, but I knew that was my goal, the destination I wanted to achieve. It was only after I removed the wall of anger and hurt I had built up, that I was open to all the good that was now flowing into my life. I became more aware of how God was working in my life each day, even in simple ways. I quit my job and tried starting my own business, but that wasn't the path that God had chosen for me. The business failed, but my faith didn't.

I was without a job, an income and hospitalization insurance when Deana came to me and told me that she had been bleeding internally. I told her to go to the doctor but she protested, saying we couldn't afford it without the hospitalization insurance. Against her wishes she went to the doctor, and when she came out she was crying. I asked her what was wrong and she said, "I don't know for sure. When he pushed in on my abdomen, I could feel something in there. What scared me most was the look on his face. He thinks I have a tumor in my colon that's causing the bleeding. He wants me to come back in a couple of days for more tests."

Later that night, even though we were watching television, I kept thinking of Deana. Suddenly the thought came into my mind, *"Pray with her."* It was the same powerful thought that I experienced in the chapel the night I was healed. I'd learned to recognize it now because it didn't come from me.

My reaction was more like, "Do what?" I felt awkward asking Deana that, not that she would have thought anything about it, but it wasn't quite my style. I sat there for three hours until the thought became so strong, I couldn't sit there anymore. Finally I said, "Deana, can I pray with you?" She said, "I'd like that." For some unknown reason, I felt compelled to pray for her with my hand over the spot where the doctor had felt the tumor. I asked her to go lie down on the bed, and as she did so, I placed my hand over her abdomen. I began to feel heat coming from my hand, but when I moved my hand further over her abdomen, I couldn't feel anything. I only felt it over one area and I couldn't understand why I felt it at all. I thought, "This is crazy. I'm supposed to be praying with her and I'm worried about feeling this heat." The thought came again and this time it was almost like a demand: *"Do it!"* Deana had been lying there with her eyes closed, and I placed my hand back over the spot where I felt the heat. I said, "Jesus, you know where I am. I don't have a job or any hospitalization insurance. I don't know what to do, but I remember somewhere in the Bible that you said, 'Whatever you ask for and believe that you have it, it will be given to you.' So, I'm asking you now that whatever it is in her abdomen that is causing her to bleed, remove it." I then had the strangest feeling. For a split second, it was as if my hand went into her abdomen. I didn't say anything about this to Deana before we went to bed.

The next night, Deana came up to me and said, "Since I have to go for the test tomorrow, would you pray with me again?" I told her I would, and as she lay there, I placed my hand over her abdomen but I couldn't feel anything. Even though I moved my hand around, I couldn't feel that heat sensation again. I tried to analyze it in my mind. Why couldn't I feel anything? Maybe she had a fever last night and that was what I felt. And then the thought came again and it said, *"You asked and it's been given you."* I can't describe how I felt. It was as if rays of heat were coming from my face and I said, "Deana, it's gone!" I just knew it to be a fact. She said, "I know. I felt something!" The next day after her test, the doctor came up to me and said, "Louis, she's fine. I don't understand it. I know what I felt but I checked all the way into her colon, as far as I could go, and she's clean as a whistle." There were no signs of bleeding, and to this day she has not had another problem.

More and more, I began to experience miracles. A friend called me and said that a friend of his had come down to Louisiana from Canada on her way to attend a convention in Atlanta, Georgia. The person who was supposed to drive her to Atlanta became ill, and my friend thought perhaps I could drive her there. I agreed, and she and Deana and I set out. It was a convention of the National Association of Clergy Hypnotherapists, and to attend you had to be a clinical hypnotherapist and an ordained minister. Our plan was to take her to the convention, then we would do a little sightseeing until it was time to pick her up. God had other plans.

When we arrived, they invited Deana and me to sit in on the convention. There were many different denominations attending. There were Baptist ministers, Methodist ministers and even Catholic priests and bishops. I was asked to share the story of how I was healed from depression, and later that afternoon Dr. Art Winkler and his wife, Dr. Pam Winkler, directors of St. John's University, approached me. They were moved by my story and suggested I study hypnotherapy. I felt that perhaps this was a way that I could help people.

I went to school, studied hypnotherapy and received my degree. I began to notice how God put certain people in my path to help me on this new journey, a journey that brought me to where I am today. And all of the trials that I experienced were merely stepping-stones, lessons I needed to learn to help me get on the right path.

When my life was filled with those negative thoughts and emotions, I was blind to all the light, goodness and love that were around me. It took my reaching the bottom of the pit before I could finally look up.

I didn't realize it back then, but that night in the chapel, in my own crude way, I was forgiving—forgiving all those who had hurt me. Through that forgiveness came my healing, freedom and true peace. It wasn't easy. I literally struggled with myself. There was a part of me that didn't want to let it go, a part of me that wanted justice or revenge because I didn't deserve what they did to me. But there was another part of me that was tired of hurting, tired of having this weight pressing down on me and overshadowing every part of my life. It would have been much easier to hold on to those negative feelings. That knot in my stomach told me that I shouldn't forgive, because I was right and they were wrong. It wasn't until I made the *choice* to pray for those who hurt me that I was open enough to allow God to come into my life and heal me in such a profound way.

Never again will I allow those things to control my life, because I know now that the choice is mine. What I want you to understand is that the choice is *yours*. Our free will, the power to choose, is the most powerful thing we have. It is so powerful that even God Himself will not interfere with it.

Most things in our lives are not life-and-death situations. But with our imagination, we blow them out of proportion. Many times we create our own mountains, our own demons. When we hear about Jesus casting out demons, many of us picture a devil with horns and fiery eyes. But the demon could be unresolved anger, resentment, bitterness, revenge, hatred or negative thinking. These demons can totally possess us, if we allow them to. We have the choice of whether or not to give them any power in our lives. There is nothing in this world that has any power over us except the power that we choose to give it.

I now realize that I suffered from more than a chemical imbalance. I suffered from an imbalance of my inner trinity—my mind, body and spirit. I didn't just suffer from it, I had caused it! I had let my mind run the same negative course over and over for so long that I became one-dimensional. I couldn't see my way around my problems because I viewed them from only one perception. Only through forgiveness was my spirit set free. And only when my spirit was truly free did I experience joy, a joy unlike anything I had ever known.

My life is filled with peace because I know the choice is mine. I have the power to control the situations in my life by choosing how I react to them.

Now that you know the power of your free will and the importance of the mind–body–spirit connection, you have taken your first step on your path to enlightenment.

In the following chapters, you will learn how the mind functions and the techniques needed to help you steer clear of negative thoughts. Set your goals clearly before you, keep your road map handy, let nothing sidetrack you from your destination, and remember that you can reach any goal you set your mind to achieve.

What you are is God's gift to you;
What you become is your gift to God.

Now your journey begins ...

Chapter 2

The Subconscious Mind

Your best friend or your worst enemy

There are few stories written about the subconscious mind. There are no songs singing its praises. There are no great movies extolling its powers. You seldom hear people speak about it. Some don't even know that it exists. And there are still others, even a few in the scientific professions, who refuse to acknowledge its awesome influence. And yet it remains the most powerful, and virtually untapped, human resource in the world!

I'm reminded of an old fable that I heard many years ago from Dr. Art Winkler. Some ancient gods were trying to decide where to hide the greatest power in the universe so that mankind would not be able to find it. One of the gods said, "Let's hide it on top of the highest mountain." They discussed that idea for a while, but decided that would not do because man would eventually climb the highest mountain and find that great power. A second god came up with the idea of hiding the greatest power at the bottom of the ocean. After another discussion among the gods, it was decided that man would someday discover a way to explore the murky depths of the ocean and the power would be discovered. Finally, a third god said, "I know what to do. Let's hide the greatest power in the universe within the mind of man. He will never think to look for it there!" And according to that old fable, they hid the greatest power in the universe within the human mind.

In my private practice as a clinical hypnotherapist, people come to me with a variety of problems, and many of them say that they've tried everything under the sun but nothing works. Smokers tell me that they've tried the nicotine patches, staples in the ear and even acupuncture, but to no avail. Those looking to reduce weight have tried every fad diet to hit the market, taken every new "miracle" pill to burn off fat, and they usually own various types of exercise equipment that now lurk deep in the closet or gather dust in some remote corner of the garage. They don't realize that the reason these things did not work is because they were all things outside of themselves. They were trying to get something else to do it for them, some magic solution. They did not succeed until they realized that they themselves possessed the power to achieve their goals all along. They're like Dorothy in *The Wizard of Oz*, who possessed the power to go home all the time. It wasn't hidden within the ruby slippers. It was within her.

As you read this book, you will have to make a decision. You may have to shift your beliefs and your attitude, and change the way you perceive yourself and others. But I can assure you, when you do this, it will have a positive and profound effect on your life. Your life will become happier, healthier, more peaceful and more productive than ever before.

The information in this book will give you the tools you will need to make these changes. For instance, if you wanted to be an electrician, you would first need to learn about electricity, wiring, switches and so on. A mechanic would need to have an understanding about the inner workings of machines, how to use the proper wrenches, screwdrivers and such. If you want to change the way you are now and become the person you *want* to be, the person God created you to be, then you also need the proper tool, which is knowledge. But first ask yourself this question: "What am I going to do with this knowledge?" Because with knowledge comes responsibility, and with responsibility comes control. Do *you* want to be in control, or do you want other people or things to control you? You are the one who must choose your place in life. Sometimes, even if a prison door is left open, the prisoner chooses not to escape. It's *your* choice. You can become the person you want to be, but you must not only want it, you must put the knowledge you gain into action. A carpenter's tools will never build a house as long as they remain in the carpenter's box. It's that simple. What you will receive from this book can change your life. *Just remember, your mind is like an umbrella. It only works when it's open.*

There's a story I once heard about an old frog that lived all of its life in a small pond, deep in the heart of the big woods. One day a new frog appeared.

"Where do you come from?" asked the old frog.

"Ah, I come from the great ocean," answered the new frog.

"The ocean?" said the old frog. "I've never seen it. Is it very big?"

"Why, it's tremendous!" exclaimed the new frog.

21

"Oh, then it must be a quarter of the size of my pond," said the old frog.

"No, it is bigger than that."

"Then it must be half as big as this pond?"

"My goodness, no. It is much larger than that!" exclaimed the new frog.

"You don't mean to tell me that it is as big as this pond?" gasped the old frog.

"It is so much larger, there is no comparison," laughed the new frog.

"That's impossible," said the frog from the pond. "I have to see this for myself."

So together they set out on a journey. The old frog had never gone beyond the confines of his own pond. When they reached the ocean, the old frog took one look and was so shocked at its immense size that his head just exploded!

The old frog simply could not comprehend the vastness of the ocean, and many times we cannot comprehend the awesome power of our own mind! We, as humans, have a tendency to make things more difficult than they are, and many times we get caught up in our own false beliefs. We, like the frog, feel that we cannot go beyond the confines of our own pond. Do you feel confined by your job or lifestyle? Perhaps you feel that what you have now is all there is. I want you to stop for a moment and ask yourself, "Am I living in a pond of my own? Am I limited because of the confines of my own false beliefs?" Do you want something better?

I would like for you to always remember this. You had no choice in coming into this world. You had no choice in who your father or mother would be. You had no choice in whether your skin would be black, white, yellow or red. You had no choice in the city, town, state or country in which you were born. You had no choice in whether you would be male or female. You may not even have had a choice in your religion. These things are your heritage and you cannot change that. However, you can change how your heritage has affected you.

Let me explain to you a little bit about the human brain and how it functions. The brain is divided into two hemispheres: the left hemisphere and the right hemisphere. The left hemisphere is the analytical part of the brain and in it are contained logic and reason. It is where scientific and number skills are developed, as well as language skills.

The right hemisphere of the brain is where creativity and ideas are born, and it is the source of imagination, feelings and emotions. Music and art awareness are also developed in this part of the brain.

There are two levels of the mind: the conscious mind and the subconscious mind. When we are functioning on the conscious level we are mainly using the left hemisphere of the brain. This part of the mind, the analytical part, is not fully developed until approximately the age of thirteen.

Although the subconscious mind seems to emanate from the right hemisphere of the brain, it is much broader and is not confined within the brain itself.

The conscious part of the mind is merely a narrowed-down version of our true existence, with the riches of the subconscious remaining virtually untapped.

The following illustration will help you to better understand the proportion of these two levels of the mind. Picture the conscious mind as literally the *tip* of the iceberg! The massive amount lying beneath the surface is the subconscious mind.

CONSCIOUS MIND

SUBCONSCIOUS MIND

God gave us a beautiful gift: the subconscious mind. Have you ever given a child a really expensive present and a few moments later found him or her playing with the box, the true gift sitting off to the side? That's what we do. We use less than 10 percent of our brain. It's like we're just playing with the box.

The subconscious mind is a very powerful part of your being. It controls all of your bodily functions. It keeps your blood circulating and your body temperature stable. It knows if there is an infection anywhere throughout your body, and it will develop thousands of white corpuscles and send them to that area to fight the invader. You are not even consciously aware that all of this is going on. You may even notice now, as you are sitting or lying down reading this book, that perhaps your legs are crossed or maybe one hand is up to your face. You did not have to make a conscious effort to cross your leg or move your hand. Your subconscious mind knew which muscles and ligaments to activate to get your hand or leg into that position. Your body is nothing more than a robot that is controlled by your subconscious mind.

But as powerful as it is, the subconscious mind cannot distinguish right from wrong, true from false or good from bad. It cannot separate reality from illusion. Everything you have ever heard, seen, smelled, tasted or experienced—every thought, secret, misunderstanding and false belief—is recorded in your subconscious mind. These impressions on the subconscious begin much farther back than you'd imagine.

After conception, cells rapidly grow and divide. These cells continue dividing, each with their individual purpose. They will form everything from the placenta, through which the fetus will receive sustenance, to life-supporting organs, such as the heart and brain.

As early as forty days after conception, brain waves can be detected and recorded. These early impulses are the beginnings of what will later control and regulate body functions, such as the circulatory and digestive systems, as soon as these structures have been formed.

By the time the fetus is seven to nine months old, it uses the four senses of vision, hearing, taste and touch. It has also experienced the difference between waking and sleeping, and it even relates to the moods and emotions of the mother. Everything that the infant experiences, not only outside of the mother but also within the womb, leaves a permanent imprint on the brain. These first imprints or perceptions are stored in the mind and can form the basis for future experiences.

Notice the word "perceptions." Perceptions are not necessarily true in reality, but instead are the way the mind *perceives* reality. These perceptions, true or false, have a profound influence on who we are and what we become. That is why it is vital to our well-being to be aware of the awesome power that lies hidden in the subconscious mind.

Research into the mind–body connection has shown that the subconscious mind can both create pain and relieve pain. It can create illness and relieve illness. I strongly believe that many illnesses are psychosomatic. The word "psychosomatic" comes from two Greek words, *psyche* (soul) and *soma* (body). The definition of "psychosomatic" is: "pertaining to, or resulting from, the interaction between the mind and body."

This is not to say that the illness is not real or that the person consciously makes a decision to be ill. But the subconscious mind, by creating an illness, is serving in the only way it knows how—by meeting the person's deepest need or expectation. Good or bad, the subconscious doesn't know the difference. Let me give you an example. Let's say that you're in an unpleasant situation and you find it difficult to make a decision to change or get out of the situation. Perhaps you're afraid of what other people will think or say. So you remain, unhappily, in that situation. You want nothing more than to get out, so the subconscious mind, in trying to meet that deepest need, can create an illness to help you achieve that purpose. It will do so even though the illness is self-destructive.

In recent years, daily life has drastically shifted toward a high-stress level. The traditional two-parent, mother-stay-at-home family has changed. There are more single-parent families. In the majority of two-parent families, both parents

are holding down full-time jobs. Some even have the responsibility of caring for aging parents. Add to this the responsibility of keeping up the house and taking the kids to soccer,
baseball and football practice, dance lessons, music lessons
and other school functions, and soon you have a time bomb
just waiting to explode. Many parents are riddled with guilt
about not spending that "quality time" with their children.
They feel that there is just not enough time in the day. They
strive to be the best mother, the best father, the best son or
daughter and then feel guilty because they don't live up to
their expectations.

In many cases, restful sleep is lost because they lie
awake at night, their minds going over what has to be done
the next day. Without realizing it, they sleep tense, ready to
tackle the next day's business, and then wonder why they
wake up feeling exhausted.

Many businesses and companies today are like pressure
cookers. They are laying off people, doubling the workload
and firing those close to retirement. Recent studies have
shown that most heart attacks occur in men on a Monday
morning between the hours of 8 and 9 a.m. Could it be job
burnout? Is the mind trying to meet that person's deepest
need? Is it creating an illness, in this case a heart attack, to
take the pressure off the body, forcing the person to take
some time for himself and giving him an excuse not to feel
guilty about taking life a little slower? Now remember, this is
not being done on a conscious level. I'm not saying that a
person consciously wants to be ill, but that the subconscious
mind will meet the deeper need.

You may wonder why a person would not want to be
healed from sickness or pain. The answer could be that there
is a secondary gain, such as sympathy, attention, admiration

or financial gain. For example, a woman involved in an automobile accident, and suffering from back pain, is waiting for a settlement from an insurance claim or lawsuit. She may want to be healed; however, on the subconscious level, she may feel that she needs her pain in order to be compensated. The deepest need and the secondary gain can be one and the same, in this case, financial gain. Or let's say a man pulls a muscle in his shoulder at work. When he comes home and tells his wife about it, she pampers him. She may massage his shoulder, bring him his supper and tend to his every need. He may not have received this kind of attention since they were first married, and he enjoys it. Who wouldn't? So on the subconscious level, he holds on to the pain to receive the secondary gain, attention. It's similar to the child who has always done well in school. His parents may both work, and since they've never had a problem with the child, they may take his success for granted. One day the child brings home a bad grade, and suddenly the parents are sitting down with the child, asking him if there's a problem. Would he like some help? Perhaps they're even visiting the school to talk with the teachers. Now the child is receiving all kinds of attention—good or bad, it doesn't matter. Now, remember, none of these things are being done intentionally; these people are not consciously aware that it is happening. Their subconscious mind is meeting their deeper needs or expectations.

The subconscious mind can be compared to a highly sophisticated computer. If you were to program into a computer that $2 + 2 = 6$, then every time you use that computer to calculate that answer, you would get the wrong answer of 6. The subconscious mind functions just like that computer because it alone cannot rationalize or analyze. *It accepts things literally!* The conscious, analytical part of the mind will say that 2 + 2 = 4, or tell you that if you touch a hot stove, you will get burned. But many times we allow false information to be programmed into the subconscious mind, and we're not even aware that it is happening.

Let me give you some common examples of this and see if any of them sound familiar. Have you ever heard someone say, "I can't quit smoking; I've been smoking for thirty years!" or "I've been on all kinds of diets and I can't lose the weight"? I'm sure you've heard the infamous remark, "I'll always be fat; it runs in my family." Or the one that I believe is number one among overweight people, "Everything I eat turns to fat; I can just look at food and gain ten pounds!"

The list of negative programming is endless. Many women come to me to help them stop smoking, and the first thing many of them say is, "I want to quit smoking but I don't want to gain weight." Some have told me, "I quit smoking about a year ago and I put on five pounds, so I went right back to smoking." I've even heard a woman remark, "My girlfriend wanted to quit smoking and I told her, 'You're going to gain weight when you quit,' and sure enough, she quit and put on ten pounds. And she never lost it!" First let me assure you of one thing: There is no relationship between smoking and weight. If there were, then everyone smoking one, two, three or even four packs of cigarettes a day should weigh no more than 120 pounds! If such a relationship did exist, why would anyone worry about going on a diet? They could just start smoking and become skinny! Look around and you will see that there are many overweight people who smoke. No, there is no relationship between smoking and weight. But if the subconscious mind accepts this false information as true, then it will meet that expectation—which, in this instance, is to gain weight. It is simply a matter of false programming.

Now, remember, every time we say something like this we are putting false information into our computer, and just like a computer, we are going to respond to it.

One of the best examples of negative programming came from a woman who told me, "It might be the death of me, but I'm going to try and make this marriage work." Instead of being something hopeful, it sounded more like a death sentence.

I am sure none of you are guilty of this type of negative programming, but I bet you know someone who is. And I can assure you that the next time you hear it, you will be aware of it!

Every day you hear people say, "I can't do that because I'm too fat (or too skinny, too tall, too short, too stupid, too ugly, too shy or too old)." *And they never will do it*, not because they can't, but because they *believe* they can't. Henry Ford once said, *"Think you can, think you can't; either way you're right."*

Our belief system is developed not only by what we tell ourselves verbally, but also by what we tell ourselves in thoughts. This is called *self-talk* and it can have either a positive effect or a profoundly negative one in your life.

I want you to take a few moments and reflect on your own self-talk. Remember comments you may have made about yourself in normal, everyday conversation. Have they been positive remarks, or are you unconsciously programming false information into your computer? What about your private thoughts? Have they been things that will help improve your life, or have they been negative suggestions that actually wear away at your self-esteem? Remember, what your mind *perceives* as truth, it will manifest into reality. *It's like a self-fulfilling prophecy!*

Unfortunately, we are not the only programmers of our subconscious. Sometimes it seems that if we haven't given ourselves a daily dose of negativity, there is always someone else eager to step in and help. Much of the false information we receive comes from things that other people have told us. Have you ever heard the comment "Gee, you look bad today"? You may have felt perfectly fine up until that point, but as the day progressed you started feeling worse. Someone planted a negative thought; you accepted it and let it grow.

Many times, without realizing it, we accept things that other people say as truth. When your subconscious mind accepts it, it may reinforce negative things you have told yourself. Once it is reinforced into your subconscious mind to a certain point, it goes into your belief system. And once it's in your belief system, you respond to what you believe in, whether it is right or wrong.

Let's take a look at our belief system and the effect it has on our lives.

31

Chapter 3

Perception + Belief =

Your Reality

Our belief system is a powerful part of our being. It decides who we are and what we become, both mentally and physically. The belief system is formed by perceptions and acceptance. When these perceptions of ourselves, whether false or true, negative or positive, are accepted as truth by our subconscious mind, they drop into our belief system and become reality. I'm sure many of you remember the famous line from the movie *Field of Dreams*, "If you build it, they will come." I would like for you to remember this: "If you believe it, it will be." Any way you do the math, it still comes out the same: *perception + belief = your reality*.

When we are first separated from our mother's womb, we become like a tape recorder, and our subconscious mind is like a blank tape, waiting to be programmed. As the analytical part of the mind is not fully developed until around age thirteen, the subconscious readily accepts and believes whatever it hears and sees as truth.

Young children have no concept of who they are. Their self-image is formed by what they've been told by others and how they perceive things to be. It can even be formed by things they've overheard. "Ooo … He's so bad!" "You look so pretty!" "You're so strong!" "You don't listen!" "She's not good at math." Think about it, what self-image are you helping to form in your child? Is it good, or is it filled with negatives? Children will live up not only to their own perceptions, but also to yours.

I recall a visit to the doctor a few years ago. Seated across the room from me was a mother with a little girl on her lap, no more than three or four years of age. Another woman leaned over and told the child that she was pretty and asked her name. The mother told her and the woman said, "That's beautiful. Where did you get that name from?" The mother replied, "My husband named her. I certainly didn't want any more kids; I had enough. So before she was born I told him that my job was to have her, and he could name her." The child was just sitting there absorbing all this information and I shuddered. What kind of self-image could she be forming? From such a simple statement, recounted over and over, a child could develop low self-esteem and the feeling of not being wanted. I can't stress enough the importance of what we say to children and around them.

If you were to tell a very young child that his hair is green, he would accept that. Then, anytime anyone would ask him what color his hair was, he would answer, "Green." That is, until he began to analyze and rationalize that information for himself. He might then say, "Mommy, you said my hair is green, but it's brown. Was it green when I was a baby?" That false perception would still be part of his belief system. Other examples of this are Santa Claus, the Easter Bunny and the Tooth Fairy. A child will believe in these until the analytical part of the brain is developed to the point that the child can analyze the information given and question their existence.

When my granddaughter Stephanie was four years old, she suffered from a bad upper respiratory infection. She was so badly congested that she was unable to sleep well, which caused her to become extremely irritable. Her crying only worsened the congestion, and my daughter was frustrated because the medicine the doctor prescribed didn't seem to help at all. She called me late that evening and asked if I could come over and see the child. When I arrived, my granddaughter was lying on the sofa and I sat down next to her. Her breathing was labored and she started to cry. "I don't feel good, Grampa." "Would you like to feel better, baby?" I asked. She nodded and I told her, "Well, you can. Do you know what I'm going to do? I'm going to give you a magic hand." I then took her little hand and cupped it within my hands and gently rubbed it. "Now, if you take your hand and put it like this, over your nose, you'll be able to breathe better, and you'll breathe so much better that you can go to sleep. Here, let's try." I took her little hand and placed her thumb on the cheek on one side of her nose, her ring finger on the other, and the two fingers in the middle went on the center of her forehead. "Now close your eyes. And as you hold your hand there, you're going to find it easier to breathe. Every time you use your magic hand, it will not only make you feel better but it will make you breathe easier. See how good it makes you feel?" Her breathing became easier, and my daughter and I went into the kitchen and left her lying there with her magic hand over her nose. When we peeked in on her a couple of minutes later, she was asleep, and she slept through the night. The next day, she placed her hand over her nose several times throughout the day and night, and her condition continued to improve.

The key is that she believed in her magic hand. She believed in it so strongly that whenever she was hurting, whether from a skinned knee or a stomachache, she would put her hand over the boo-boo and it didn't hurt anymore. Whenever anyone in the family didn't feel well, she'd try to comfort them with her magic hand. She even tried to give a magic hand to each child in her kindergarten class. As she grew up, whenever she had a cold, you would see her sitting there with her hand over her nose and her eyes closed, and it always seemed to help her.

Just recently, while visiting my daughter, my grand-daughter complained of a runny nose. I told her, "Why don't you use your magic hand?" "It doesn't work anymore, Grandpa," she said. It took me by surprise for a moment and I realized that, at age fourteen, she had lost some of that childlike faith and belief and it saddened me. Up until that point she had perceived that she had a magic hand, and she believed in it so strongly that it created a reality. It wasn't until she began to analyze, or perhaps someone told her that there was no such thing, that she lost that belief.

As children, our faith is boundless. Anything is possible and we can do anything. But something happens when the conscious mind fully matures. We become skeptical and fearful. We begin to set boundaries to our imagination and limits to what we can do. Yes, it's sad when we lose our magic hand.

Her magic hand worked for her because she believed in it so strongly. This is a prime example of the *placebo effect*.

36

The word "placebo" comes from the Latin word meaning "I will please." It is a medication or treatment that seems thera-peutic, but is actually void of any active pharmacological substance. It will only work if the person believes that it will. It is often used for control (comparison) groups in clinical trials or studies of new medications. Before the study, the patients are told that they might be given a placebo. The patients do not know if they received the actual medication or merely a placebo.

On average, 35 percent of patients who receive place-bos report satisfactory results even though they received no active medication. The placebo is another example of the mind meeting the patients' expectations. If they expect it to help them, it will. The placebo is documented proof of the mind's ability to heal the body when the person believes it is capable of doing so.

In the same way that a placebo can have a positive effect on the body, it can also cause a negative event called the *nocebo effect*. The nocebo is a negative expectation, and many times it can be caused by health care professionals. Have you ever needed a blood test or an injection? Normally, the last thing you hear before the needle is inserted is, "Now, this is going to hurt." And it usually does. This is an example of the nocebo effect. The negative expectation produced the negative effect that was expected.

Cancer patients are usually forewarned of the effects of chemotherapy, such as hair loss, fatigue, nausea, etc. Why do some people who receive this kind of treatment experience these symptoms, while others don't? Could it be that the sug-gestion of negative symptoms created that response? In one controlled study by the British Stomach Cancer Group, 30 percent of the placebo-treated group lost their hair and

56 percent of the same group had "drug-related" nausea or vomiting. There was no pharmacological reason why they should have experienced these symptoms. It was merely that they expected the symptoms, they believed they would occur, and so they occurred.

If we accept the fact that the body heals itself of minor wounds and injuries, why do we find it so hard to believe that it can also rid itself of serious disease or illness? God created us with everything we need to exist in life. He created man and woman, not the corner drugstore. I believe that is what Jesus meant when he said, "Whatever you ask for in prayer and believe that you have, it will be given unto you" (Matthew 21:22).

Did you know that the word "believe" and its variations are mentioned approximately 111 times in the New Testament alone? When Jesus saw people who were blind, crippled or full of sores, he felt a deep compassion for them. But he didn't go up to everyone on the street corner and say, "Would you like to see?" "Would you like to get up and walk?" "Would you like to get rid of all those sores on your body?" It was only the ones who came up to him, those who stepped out in faith and believed in him, who were healed. When Jesus healed, he didn't zap the person with a lightning bolt from the heavens. He said simply, "Go, your faith has healed you." *Your faith!* Isn't it possible that Jesus wanted us to realize the wonderful gift his Father had given each of us? In Luke 17:21, Jesus said that the kingdom of God is within you. I believe that he was trying to tell us that the answers we need aren't "out there" somewhere. God created us with everything we need to be happy and whole, and it lies within each of us. It was put there when your soul first came into existence. This is where the answer is to all of our questions.

This is where the solution is to all of our problems. And this is where our true happiness and peace abide.

Hopefully, by now, you are beginning to realize the impact that your belief system has on your well-being. Remember, your perceptions play a large part in forming your beliefs. This is probably the major reason that Jesus could not perform many miracles in his own hometown (Matthew 13:53-58). These people had a certain perception of Jesus that hindered their belief. To them this was simply Jesus, the carpenter's son, the boy they studied with and played marbles with. In their eyes he was no different than they were. Their perceptions prevented them from experiencing miracles.

A dear friend, Sheila, shared with me an example of how perceptions can actually hinder the healing process. Her father had been hospitalized when the doctors discovered five blood clots in his head. After a great deal of examination, the doctors felt sure that these clots would dissolve back into his system. They released him with the instructions that he was to eat well, get plenty of rest, try some light exercise such as walking, and be sure to have someone with him twenty-four hours a day. They expected nothing but improvement and wanted to see him in two weeks.

Sheila brought her father home, but within two days she felt she was slowly watching him die. She couldn't get him to eat. He didn't want to walk. He could hardly even make it to the bathroom. And each day she watched him become weaker and weaker. She considered taking him back to the hospital, but he refused because he wanted to stay home.

She was extremely close to her father and didn't know what to do to help him. She said, "I prayed to God and told Him that I didn't want to lose my father. I didn't want to let him go. But if it was His will for my father to die now, I would let him go. And you know, Louie, it was as if the Lord said to me, 'Then you have to tell him, because he thinks he's going to die.' I thought, 'I don't know what to say. I don't know what to do.' But that evening I decided to talk to him. I sat beside him and said, 'Dad, can you hear me? Are you listening to me?' and he nodded yes. 'Daddy, you've got to listen to me. You're not going to die. You're going to live, if that's what you want to do. The doctors said you're going to live and that the blood clots would dissolve. They sent you home to heal. I don't want you to die, Daddy, but if that's what you want, I'll let you go. I want you to know, though, that I love you and I want you to live. But you've got to choose. If you want to live, you're going to have to try. You're going to have to eat. And you're going to have to get up and move around if you want to live. As much as I want it, I can't do those things for you. You're going to have to do it for yourself. I understand that you're tired and I know that you don't feel well, but if you want to live, you're going to have to do it. Daddy, you're not going to die unless *you* want to die. It's up to *you*. I want you to tell me, right now, what it is that *you* want. Do you want to live or do you want to die?' He looked at me and said, 'I want to live.' 'Then you're going to have to do it, Daddy.' Do you know, he got up, went to the table and ate everything on his plate. He started walking with me, and the next day he rode with me on the tractor and even drove it a little. In less than two weeks he was back at work, and at his two-week check, the blood clots were dissolved."

Her father's perception that his life was over almost became his reality. Unfortunately, many times people do not realize how powerful and destructive these false perceptions can be. To improve your life, you must improve the way you perceive life.

Many times, as adults, we are still responding to false perceptions we formed as children. A few years ago, a client came to me because he never felt loved or needed. He was a successful man, but no matter how much he achieved, he still felt terrible about himself. During one of his sessions, he said he felt like he was in his mother's womb. He could hear his mother and father arguing. His father then slapped his mother and said, "I'm getting the hell out of here," and he left. I asked him if his parents were divorced, and he said no. After his sessions, he told me he realized that all this time he had thought that his parents didn't want him. But they had never said anything like that to him. It was just the way he had perceived it. Whether the incident was something he imagined or whether it was an imprint before birth, didn't matter. Once he became aware of what was causing the problem, he was able to overcome it.

Deep-rooted false perceptions are the reason many abused men and women stay with their spouses. Abused people are usually bombarded with negative programming that leaves them totally lacking any form of self-esteem. They remain in the situation because they begin to believe what they've been told—that they're not good enough, smart enough, pretty enough. They don't deserve anything because they're not worth anything. They strive harder and harder to make themselves be accepted and loved. They try to be the best wife, lover, mother, go-getter, nurse, cook and house-keeper, and yet seem to fall short every time. False perceptions will keep them living a life of misery.

People suffering from anorexia can actually die from a false perception. They can look in the mirror, weighing only seventy pounds and literally starving to death, and still see themselves as fat. Why? It's because the mind controls the vision. If they perceive themselves as fat, then that is what they are going to see.

I recall a story I heard about a woman with a defective nose. When she was a child, everyone made fun of her. At school, she endured incessant teasing about her nose and she swore that when she grew up, if she ever got enough money, she would have corrective surgery. When she grew up, she went to one of the best plastic surgeons available and had the surgery done on her nose. A week or so after the surgery, the doctor came into her room and told her that he was ready to take off the bandages. He removed the bandages and told her that the surgery was a great success. He handed her the mirror, but when she looked in it she turned to him and said sadly, "But I'm still ugly." Even though the physical changes had taken place, she still perceived herself as being ugly. More than needing to correct her nose, she needed to correct her perceptions.

Unfortunately, people have the tendency to believe the worst because it's easy to believe the worst. Have you seen the bumper sticker "Life's a bitch and then you die"? I cringe every time I see that one. Can you imagine the type of life people have if they really believe that concept? Sometimes people get so wrapped up in their problems, they can't see a solution. For them, the only light at the end of the tunnel is an oncoming locomotive. But by changing their attitude and the way they perceive things, they can burst forth into the light and rise above their problems. The problems may still be there, but they are no longer beaten down by them.

Let me share with you the story of two little boys. One of them was a pessimist and the other was an optimist. Their father was concerned because no matter what happened, the little boy who was pessimistic was never happy. He seemed to find fault in everything. On the other hand, the father was also concerned about the child who was an optimist. He feared that this child had a problem facing reality because no matter how bad the situation, the child always found something good about it. The father felt that each child should be well-balanced, and one day he devised a plan to try to equal out the boys' personalities. When the boys arrived home from school, the father took the boy who was a pessimist and brought him to his room. In it, he had placed every kind of toy and game a child could want. There were video games, skates, scooters, action heroes and toys of every kind. He told the boy that it was all his and he wanted him to have a good time. He closed the door and went to get his other son. He brought the optimistic son to his room, but when he opened the door, all of the child's belongings had been removed. In the center of the room was a large pile of horse manure that went from the floor to the ceiling. He put the child in the room and quietly closed the door.

After a while, he went up to check on their progress. The pessimistic child was sitting in the middle of the floor, crying. "What's wrong?" asked the father. "Everything," said the boy. "I was playing with those action heroes and one of them has a loose arm. And I hate that stupid video game because I can't beat it. I'm afraid to try the scooter, because I might fall off and hurt myself. It's just not fair." The father couldn't believe it and left the child sitting there crying. When he got close to the optimist's room, he could hear laughing and shouting. He opened the door and couldn't believe what he saw. There was his son, covered from head to toe in horse manure, laughing and digging on top of the smelly mound. "Son!" he shouted. "What *are* you doing?" "Dad," the boy shouted in excitement, "with all this manure, there must be a pony in here somewhere!"

Optimism is a prescription for healing. By developing a more optimistic outlook, a person is more likely to overcome pain and adversity because their main focus is no longer on the problem at hand. For example, optimistic surgery patients generally recover more quickly and have fewer post-operative complications than those who are less hopeful. One surgeon told me that 80 percent of a person's recovery depended on the patient's attitude going into surgery. Those with a positive attitude and faith in their doctor had less pain, less bleeding, a quicker recovery and a shorter stay in the hospital.

Why do some patients live longer than others given the same diagnosis? Could the difference be their attitude? A man came to me several years ago and told me he had been diagnosed with cancer and only had about six months to live. He said, "I told the doctor, 'Like hell! I understand that if God takes me, fine. But I'm going to beat this damn cancer!'" His dream was to spend his retirement traveling with his wife, so after his diagnosis, he bought a motor home and set out. This man was determined that the illness wasn't going to be his death sentence. That's probably why his six months turned into a few years.

No story seems to illustrate this point better than the story of my mother-in-law, Georgia. She was a wonderful woman who in 1944 found out she had uterine cancer. The doctors, at that time, told her the only thing they could do was treat it with radium. It was a new procedure that wasn't perfected yet, but they didn't have anything else. She looked at the doctor and said, "Doggone it! I'm going to beat this thing. I have three good reasons. One is ten, one is eight and one is six." (She was talking about her three children.) She took the treatments faithfully, had a positive outlook and eventually beat the cancer.

She went back for yearly checkups, and in 1981, after thirty-seven years, they told her she had cancer in the same area. This time it was fused to her colon. The doctors said it required surgery, but didn't give her much hope of pulling through because she also had emphysema. When my wife spoke to her, Georgia was positive and upbeat. "Look, I beat it before, doggone it, I'll beat it again!" She had the surgery, and against the odds, she was cured.

Four years later, in 1985, she was diagnosed with lung cancer. She was seventy years old. The doctor said that they couldn't operate because the emphysema was worse and she wouldn't make it through the surgery or anesthesia. The good thing was that the spot on her lung was so tiny, he felt that radiation would work well. After all, it had worked well for her on a much worse cancer.

A week later, she flew down to visit with us and stayed for three weeks. One day, she and my wife were talking. "Deana, I won't be back to Louisiana." "What do you mean, Mom?" "I'm not going to live past seventy-one," she replied. My wife was taken aback and questioned her further. "Mom, why would you say something like that? The doctor seems to think that you'd be fine after treatments." "No, I'm not going to live longer than that. No one in my family ever lived past seventy-one." She truly believed that, and nothing my wife said could change her mind.

She went home and began her treatments. The following April, Georgia celebrated her seventy-first birthday.

When she completed her treatments, the doctors told

her that they had been unable to get it all. They had done all they could.

My wife went to stay with her for a few months. The last time Deana took her to the doctor's office, he gave her a death sentence. He told her, "Georgia, there isn't anything else we can do for you except put you in the hospital and keep you comfortable. You are going to die and you don't have six months to live. In fact, you don't even have two months left. It's probably no more than three weeks." She told him that if she had to die, she wanted to die at home.

When she and Deana came out of the doctor's office, Georgia turned to her niece, Molly, and said, "There's no hope."

Up until that point, she had been doing pretty well and enjoying life as much as possible. But suddenly, it was as if she had given up completely.

Three weeks later, on October 30, she died at the age of seventy-one.

Georgia already had a very strong false belief that people in her family didn't live past a certain age, and the negative prognosis given by her doctor only reinforced that false belief. Once she accepted it, it determined her quality and length of life.

Many doctors do not realize the tremendous impact a prognosis of doom and gloom has on a patient. In his book *Love, Medicine and Miracles*, Dr. Bernie Siegel says, "I find the word 'terminal' terribly upsetting. It means that a doctor is treating the person as though he or she is already dead."

And in *Peace, Love and Healing*, Dr. Siegel says, "We kill people by saying a disease is 100 percent fatal."

One of my favorite stories is the one he tells about a woman whose oncologist told her that she only had about a year to live. She fired him, went to a new oncologist with the warning, "I just fired my last doctor. So please keep your guesses to yourself because I will beat this thing."

I believe it is vitally important for people to remember that when a doctor gives this type of prognosis it is merely an educated guess. It does not have to be accepted as a death sentence.

I have recommended these books by Dr. Bernie Siegel many times to my clients because I feel they can be a life-saver by helping people to realize the important role they themselves play in their own healing process.

As long as people have hope, something to look forward to or something to accomplish, it gives them a goal to focus on instead of focusing on the illness, thus improving their chances of recovery.

One day a dear friend called to let us know that her brother, Henry, was going into surgery to have part of his lung removed. He was in his late sixties and she was understandably worried that he might not come through the surgery. She said, "I wish there was something we could do to help him." I told her, "We'll definitely keep him in our prayers. But along with the prayers, why don't you give him something to look forward to? Doesn't he enjoy going places and going on trips?" "Oh yes, he loves it," she replied. "Then why not plan a trip for after the surgery. Give him something to look forward to, something to be excited about, so that he sees something beyond the surgery."

They planned a trip to Florida and kept reinforcing what a great time they would all have. Another thing Henry had going for him was his fantastic attitude. He didn't dwell on the surgery or fill his mind with what-ifs.

He came through the surgery with flying colors. Everyone, including the doctors and hospital staff, was amazed with how quickly he recovered and Henry finally went on that trip to Florida. He enjoyed good health for many years after that.

Mental attitude is vitally important in the recovery process, and keeping some goal or dream in mind helps to maintain the focus on something other than the surgery or illness at hand. Remember, there's always a trip to take, a dance to be danced, a song to be sung, a book to be written, a relationship to be built, a hug to be shared or a goal to achieve.

Some people believe that it is God's will for them to be sick. If it was God's will for people to be sick, then when Jesus came, he went against his Father's will because he healed people. If we truly believe that it is God's will for us to be sick, why do we go to doctors? Why do we take an aspirin for a headache? Are we purposely going against God? Are we trying to fool Him? Not at all. And if it is not God's will for us to have a headache, at what level does it become God's will for us to be sick? Is it God's will for us to have cancer? Of course not! In John 10:10, Jesus said, "I have come to give you life and give it more abundantly." Nowhere in the entire New Testament did Jesus ever say, "It is better for you to be sick." A good example of this is in Mark 1:40-42. A leper came to Jesus and, kneeling down, begged him and said, "If you wish, you can make me clean." Moved with pity, Jesus stretched out his hand, touched him and said to him, "I do will it. Be made clean." Immediately, the leprosy left him and he was made clean.

Our loving Father does not desire us to have illness. Sometimes these things happen. They are a part of life.

John 9:1-3 states, "As he passed by he saw a man blind from birth. His disciples asked him 'Rabbi, who sinned, this man or his parents, that he was born blind?' Jesus answered, 'Neither he nor his parents sinned; it is so that the works of God might be made visible through him." It wasn't through any fault of the blind man that he couldn't see and it wasn't a punishment, either. It is the same with us when we are faced with illness or disease. We can change the way we view illness and instead use these adversities to grow spiritually.

When we change the way we perceive illness, we remove feelings of hopelessness that can hinder the healing process. An inhalation therapist who worked at a local hospital shared this story with me. During her treatment rounds, she stopped at the room of a patient scheduled for a breathing treatment. She remembered him from a couple of previous stays in the hospital. He was about fifty years old, ex-Navy and spunky. When she entered the room he smiled and said, "Well, c'mon in. You better hurry up and give me that treatment, 'cause I'm fixin' to go home." She asked him how long he'd been there and he told her two weeks. She said, "Well, good. You must be doing better." "I'm doing great," he said, "not bad for a dead man." She was a little taken aback and asked him what he meant. "Well," he said, "the doctor told me that I had lung cancer and I probably only had another six or eight months to live. So I told him he was full of it. That was five years ago." He laughed, "So I guess I'm doing great for a dead man!"

He didn't accept the death sentence given to him. He never gave up hope. You see, there is no such thing as false hope. Any hope is true hope and it can change one's belief system, thus allowing healing to take place.

In much the same way that optimism can be beneficial, pessimism seems to aggravate ill health. One long-term study showed that people who were pessimistic have significantly higher rates of illness through their middle age. They are also prone to depression and have a greater tendency toward shorter life spans than optimistic people.

Think about someone you know who is pessimistic. A simple "Hello, how are you?" turns into a thirty-minute monologue on every little ache and pain and problem they are experiencing. People who are pessimistic always seem to have more than their share of illnesses and troubles. Listen to them long enough, and soon you begin to feel down and depressed too.

Just like the common cold, optimism and pessimism are contagious. Think about it. Everyone wants to be around optimists. They are generally happier and more fun-loving, and it feels good just to be around them. Almost everyone knows someone in the pessimist category. They're always gloomy, suffer from every malady known to man and feel it their duty to share it with you. When you see them out somewhere, you try to pretend you didn't because after talking to them for a while, you're down in the dumps too.

We seem to develop a tendency toward optimism or pessimism at an early age. However, by shifting your perceptions, you can develop a more optimistic way of thinking, which will improve your health and well-being and even have a positive effect on others around you, regardless of your age.

To change your perceptions, you have to see yourself the way you want to be. When I say "see," I mean literally see it. Close your eyes and envision it down to the last minute detail. Some people may not be visual and able to see that picture, and that's fine. Instead, think about it being the way you want. Imagine, pretend—whatever works for you. When you have that clear mental image of how you want to be, hold on to it, lock it into your memory and refer to it often. Begin to think of yourself that way and it will be easy for you to make the changes necessary to achieve your goal. For example, smokers need to see themselves as non-smokers, enjoying life without being chained to a cigarette. They need to see themselves breathing easier, being able to run without becoming winded, feeling better about their appearance, and noticing how their teeth will be whiter, their breath fresher-smelling and their fingernails getting clearer, without the yellow stain caused by smoking. Overweight people must begin to think of themselves as thin—thinking how good it feels not to be carrying around that extra weight, and noticing how much more energy they have, how much easier it is to breathe. They need to see themselves enjoying being thin—going to the beach, buying new clothes, noticing how good they feel about themselves.

Being able to visualize your goal is a large part of achieving it. In one of my classes at St. John's University, Dr. Art Winkler described research that was done at UCLA involving 200 students who had never played basketball. They were divided into two groups. One group went to the gym daily and practiced free shots, while the other group was hypnotized and only imagined practicing free shots. The group that was hypnotized and visualized doing the free shots actually made more baskets than the group that only physically practiced them. The ones who visualized it never missed a basket in their mind; thus it built up their confidence. The ones who only practiced the free shots physically, however, developed a negative imprint each time they missed a shot.

World champion athletes will tell you that when they trained, they saw themselves as winning. I remember a television interview in which the reporter asked a professional skater what she attributed her success to. The skater said she practiced, of course, but each day she spent time going over her routine in her mind. She said she went over each and every detail. She could feel herself doing the routine, picking up speed, going into the jumps, coming down and landing her skate on the ice. She said that when she imagines herself doing it, she doesn't fall. She never saw herself failing. Because she had gone over it so much in her mind, when she got out on the ice it was all very natural for her.

A while back, my granddaughter Tammy called me because her softball team was experiencing a slump. She asked if there was anything I could do that would help the team overcome the rut they were in. I explained to her the importance of first visualizing the outcome they wanted, seeing themselves as winners. I offered to talk to the team and they agreed.

During the talk, I explained to them how the subconscious mind functions and then did visualization techniques with the team members. I told them how important it was to first see themselves as winning, see themselves hitting that home run, see themselves catching that ball, etc. I told them if they could perceive it and believe it, they could achieve it.

Afterwards, I told Tammy that if she wanted me to do a private session with her to help improve her batting, I would.

During the session, I told her that when she stepped out onto the field, before she even stepped up to the plate, to first look off in the distance beyond the fence. Pick a tree, any tree she saw that caught her attention. This tree was *her* tree. I told her to visualize the pitcher throwing the ball. She could see the ball coming in to the plate. She could see herself swinging the bat and hear a crack as the bat made contact with the ball. And every time she swung, she could see the ball sailing out of the field and hitting her tree. I told her to use this visualization technique often.

After the session, I shared with her a visualization experiment that I had done. One evening, I decided to conduct a small experiment using a visualization technique. I took a fork out of our kitchen drawer and went into my office. It was a standard piece of stainless flatware, about one-eighth of an inch thick. I'm not a muscular man, but I knew that if I tried I could probably bend it in half. But twisting it around was another matter.

I held the fork with both hands and closed my eyes. I visualized the metal part between my two thumbs getting hot. I imagined it getting hotter and hotter and even beginning to glow red. In my mind, I visualized the metal growing more and more red and beginning to soften. I imagined it becoming softer and more pliable until suddenly I knew it was soft enough to twist. Without another thought or moment's hesitation, I twisted my wrists. When I opened my eyes, I was surprised to see that I didn't just bend the fork, but I actually corkscrewed the handle! I was excited and went to the kitchen to try it again. This time I picked up a large tablespoon. It was almost twice as thick as the fork, and the first thing I thought was, "I don't know if I could twist this because it's much thicker than the fork." Mistake number one: I had entertained doubt.

Using the same technique as before, I tried to visualize the metal getting soft, but each time I did, I remembered how thick it was. It took me much longer to visualize it becoming soft because of one fleeting negative thought I had experienced earlier. I pushed the thought out of my mind and continued to focus on the metal becoming hot. As before, I visualized it getting softer and softer until I knew it was at the point of pliability. I twisted it and instantly remembered the thickness. It twisted, but not to the extent that the fork did.

This is a photo of the fork and spoon I twisted.

I was impressed with the results, but my wife did not share that same enthusiasm when I showed her the good flatware. Neither did she find it amusing when I tried to explain that they were still usable, they just had a small twist in the handle!

My granddaughter was excited as I pulled the fork and spoon out of the desk drawer. She left that day, inspired and amazed.

A couple of days later, Tammy came to my house and excitedly held out a fork that she had also twisted. She explained that in school recently they had heated glass tubes until they were soft enough to be either stretched or twisted into shapes. So when she tried her experiment, she visualized the fork being heated over a burner like the ones at school until it got soft enough to bend, and then she twisted it.

I was excited for her and asked her where she had gotten the fork. "Oh, it was one of Mom's." After she left I called my son's house and he answered. "Look, Louie, I want to tell you what happened," I said. I proceeded to tell him about the talk I had with his daughter and about her little "experiment." "Louie, she's excited and probably going to come to you and tell you what she did. I just didn't want you to be shocked and come down too hard on her about the fork. Don't take away what she accomplished and don't tell her I talked to you. Let her tell you about it." He said, "Okay, Dad, I understand."

About a week later, he called and said, "Dad, Tammy still hasn't come to us about taking the fork, so we went to her room to see if we could find it. What we found instead were two more forks and a couple of spoons, so would you please tell her to come tell us about it because we're running out of things to eat with!"

I worked that incident out with my granddaughter, and that season not only did her batting improve but her team broke out of their slump and made it to the state playoffs.

It's all a matter of perception. If you perceive yourself as winning, you'll win, and if you perceive yourself as failing, it's almost a sure bet that you'll fail.

Perception is powerful and it can control your life. Just remember, *you* can control the perception.

Try the following exercises to help you better understand perception and the different ways we view things.

Read this sentence:

FINISH FILES ARE THE RESULT OF YEARS OF SCIENTIFIC STUDY COMBINED WITH THE EXPERIENCE OF MANY YEARS.

Without looking at it again, think about how many F's were contained in the sentence. Take your time.

Having a little trouble? Read it again. Now how many F's did you see? Did you see three? How about four? Did you see five? There are actually six F's in the sentence.

Even after reading it a second time, most people still do not see the correct number of F's in the sentence, but because they are so sure they did, they will aggressively argue with me that they "know what they saw." It's a humbling experience to recognize that we can still be mistaken after looking at the same thing two or three times.

Sometimes people look at the same thing, but not in the same way. Take, for example, the following pictures. What do *you* see?

Do you see a horse?

Turn the picture slightly. Do you still see a horse, or do you see a frog?

How about this one? Do you see an old woman?

Or do you see a young woman?

Look at this picture. Do you see a goblet?

Or do you see two faces?

Just as there is more than one way to view these pictures, there is more than one way to view the situations in your life. How you view these situations will be the determining factor in how these situations affect you.

But just as important as how we view life, is how we view ourselves. Many times we allow false perceptions to create a poor self-image. What is your self-image? How do you perceive yourself? Do you see yourself as inadequate? unworthy? ugly? Do you see yourself as a failure? Do you feel insecure?

In Matthew 22:34-40, Jesus was asked which is the greatest commandment. He said, "You must love your God with all your heart, with all your soul and with all your mind. This is the first and greatest commandment. The second is like it. You shall love your neighbor as yourself."

Many times, if we loved our neighbors as we love ourselves, our neighbors would be in terrible shape! He was telling us that we need to love ourselves the way God created us. In order to love your neighbor, you must first love yourself. If you want to give time to others, first take some time for yourself and don't feel guilty about it. If you want to give money to the poor, you must first have money. You can't give what you don't have.

We must learn to love ourselves and get rid of many of the negative perceptions we have. Remember, these negative perceptions can be false, but if left unchanged, they will create a negative reality.

I want you to look at it from a new perspective. I want you to see yourself as God sees you. Remember the old saying "You can't judge a book by its cover"? An infinite amount of wisdom is contained within these words.

As humans, we have a tendency to judge things only with our eyes. And as we learned in the previous exercise, that leaves a lot of room for mistakes. God has a greater depth of vision and He sees beyond our faults and blemishes.

In I Samuel 16:7 the Lord said to Samuel, "Do not judge from his appearance or from his lofty stature, because I have rejected him. Not as man sees does God see, because man sees the appearance but the Lord looks into the heart."

God created you with many talents, many abilities and many blessings. You were made in His image and likeness and there is an inner beauty in all of us. But you may have allowed this truth to be covered over with false perceptions.

To illustrate this point further, take a look at this picture of a geode.

What do you see?

If you were to judge the geode by its outward appearance alone, it would seem of little value. At first glance, you would perceive this as nothing more than a mere rock, just like hundreds of others you've seen in your lifetime: rough, unattractive, unwanted and easily discarded.

You must go beyond what the eyes perceive to discover the true crystalline beauty hidden within:

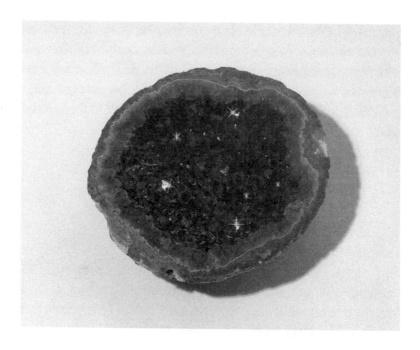

It is much the same with us. Once you break through the false perceptions you have of yourself and others, you will discover that inner treasure that lies hidden within each of us.

I would recommend that you purchase a geode or find a full-color picture that does justice to its awesome beauty. It's proven to be an invaluable tool as a reminder that true beauty is not always easy to recognize and that we are all created special and unique. We must develop a new perception and learn to see ourselves as our heavenly Father sees us.

Jesus said, "The kingdom of God is within you." It's not only in those who attend church every Sunday. It's not only in those who don't take drugs. And it's not only in those who don't steal or lie or cheat. But the kingdom of God is within every person, regardless of what they've done. And that means that every person is capable of experiencing physical, mental, emotional and spiritual healing.

It reminds me of the story of the eagle and the chicken. Once there was an eagle that was getting ready to give birth. She built a nest on top of a beautiful, majestic mountain and there she laid her eggs. One day, as she flew off in search of food, one of the eggs rolled out of the nest. It tumbled down onto some pine straw, so it didn't break. It just kept gradually rolling down the hillside and soon it stopped along the fence of a farmer's property. It just so happened that the farmer was checking his fence line that day and he came upon the egg. He held it in his hand, not knowing what type of egg it was, and thought perhaps there was some chance of saving it. So he brought it home and put it in his chicken coop next to the chicken eggs. The hens sat on the eagle's egg just as they did their own, and after some time had passed, the eggs hatched. The little chicks started chirping, so the little eagle began chirping. As the chicks got a little stronger, they jumped out of the nest; so too did the eagle. The little chickens began to walk around, scratching the ground and pulling worms out of the mud. The little eagle tried to do the same, but he had some trouble because his beak was different. The other chickens made fun of him, but he was persistent and soon he too got a worm. One day, the chickens flapped their wings and flew about four feet off the ground and ten feet in distance. The little eagle saw this and flapped his wings, and he too flew the same height and distance. Time passed, and one day the little eagle was in the yard by himself and happened to look up. In the sky he saw this beautiful, majestic bird with a four-foot wingspan, gliding on the warm currents of the air with no effort. It was so beautiful and he was so amazed that he called to all the little chickens and said, "Look! Look! What is that?" And the chickens said, "Oh, that's an eagle. It belongs to the sky. It's unlimited. But we're chickens and we belong to the earth. We do not go beyond the limits of our yard." Not long after that, the little eagle died, still believing he was a chicken.

Don't let this happen to you. Don't allow false beliefs to stop you from being the person God created you to be. Go beyond the limits you have set for yourself and don't sit around, waiting until it's too late.

There could be another ending to this story and it goes like this: The little eagle looked up in sky and saw a beautiful, majestic bird. As he stared at it in amazement, the big eagle looked down and saw the little eagle in the chicken pen and wondered what he was doing there. The majestic eagle swooped down and stood alongside the little eagle. "Who are you?" asked the little eagle. "I am an eagle," he said. "Who are you?" "I am a chicken," replied the little eagle. The big eagle straightened his shoulders, pulled his wings forward and said, "A chicken? Look at my claws and look at yours. They are the same. Now look at my beak. It is the same as yours. Do you see my eyes? Our eyes are the same." The big eagle then spread out his wings. "Open your wings. See, they are the same as mine. You are not a chicken, you are an eagle. Come, fly with me." Up into the air they flew, high above the chicken coop, far beyond the limits of the yard and far beyond all the things of the past. And the little eagle became what God created him to be.

No one can predict to what heights you can soar;
Even you will not know until you spread your wings.

Chapter 4

The Power of a Thought

"As a man thinketh, so shall he be."

If you want to change your life, you must first learn to change your thoughts. Did you know that in the past few hours you may have had a negative thought or attitude that, if entertained, could weaken your immune system and cause you to develop an unwanted health problem? It could even affect you mentally and emotionally and cause depression. But did you also know that in the past few hours you may have had a positive thought or attitude that, if entertained, could strengthen your immune system and protect you from illness and disease and give you peace of mind and happiness?

Most people do not realize that a mere thought has the ability to bring about physical changes in the body. But the mere thought of an embarrassing moment can cause the blood to rush to the face, creating a blush. Just thinking of certain sexual situations can cause arousal in men and women. The thought of some creepy, crawly bug can literally cause the skin to itch, and someone merely thinking about their deepest fear may experience a racing of the heart and rapid breathing. Yes, a mere thought can be very powerful indeed!

Thoughts come into your mind constantly. While you are reading this book, watching television, before you fall asleep or at any time throughout the day, a thought may come into your mind. It could be a good thought, a bad thought or even an evil thought. You have to understand that it is okay to have that thought, because you had no control over where that thought came from. However, once the thought is in your mind, then you have control over it. You can accept it or reject it. Entertain it or dismiss it. That's called *free will*. Our free will is probably one of the greatest gifts God ever gave us. It is so powerful that even God Himself does not interfere with it. By your free will, you choose how the thought will affect you. Many times when people pray, they ask God to take away their hurt or their anger or their pain. But God doesn't take away what you are not willing to give up. You must be willing to let it go.

Next time you begin to feel upset, angry, overwhelmed, depressed or uncomfortable, stop and look at your thought process. What are you thinking at that moment? If what you are thinking is negative, you will produce negative results.

When I was young, I had an old phonograph. I would sit for hours playing those old records and listening to my favorite songs. But after so long, some of the records would develop a scratch. Every time I would play them, when it reached that certain point, the record would skip and repeat the same phrase over and over again. Listening to the same thing over and over again was nerve-wracking. It would keep going on and on until I had enough and would bump the phonograph to make it stop. Many times when we have a negative thought, it becomes just like that old record. We play it over and over again in our mind until finally we just can't seem to take it anymore. It literally begins to affect every aspect of our lives. That's exactly what happened to me. I played those negative thoughts over and over again in my mind until finally it created a chemical imbalance and depression. My mind was able to do that because I was not aware of what was happening.

I can assure you that after reading this book, you will have a protective shield around you. Once you learn about the mind and how it functions, and understand the power of perceptions and thoughts, you will achieve a new awareness. This awareness will become your protective shield. You may want to call it your *awareness shield.*

Many times we are surrounded by negative energy. Maybe it's from negative thoughts or false perceptions, or perhaps it's from something that someone said to you. It may even be caused by something from your past. It doesn't matter. From now on, whenever you are bombarded by this negative energy, instead of it affecting you and causing you to lose control and respond spontaneously, it will hit your awareness shield. You will see it for what it is. You will know that if you continue to entertain this negative thought, you will experience the negative results it will bring you: It's going to make you feel angry, depressed, bitter, deprived, inadequate or ill. Once you have this awareness, you can say to that thought, "*NO!* I refuse to accept you anymore. You have controlled my way of life long enough!" And as you do this, that negative thought or energy will vanish, because it is only an illusion. It only has the power that you give it.

Most things in our lives are not life-and-death situations, but through the process of our thoughts and imagination, we blow them way out of proportion. Shakespeare once said, "There is nothing either good or bad, but thinking makes it so." If you think the world is caving in on you, it's certainly going to feel that way.

Our thoughts are very powerful. If you take a thought, good or bad, you can manifest it into reality. It's like a self-fulfilling prophecy.

When our thoughts are negative and in confusion, we create an unreal world. If you have thoughts of how unfairly you've been treated, you will perceive a world full of unfairness. If you have thoughts of suspicion, you will perceive a suspicious world. If your thoughts are fearful, you will perceive a fearful world. How can you expect your spirit to soar when it's weighted down by suspicion, resentment, self-pity, anger and unfairness? But if your thoughts are positive, you will look out on a world full of mercy and love. Your spirit will soar with joy and your life will be peaceful.

It's a law of the universe. Some call it karma. The Bible states, "As you sow, so shall you reap." What type of seeds have you been planting in the rich, fertile soil of your mind? If you plant a seed of corn, it won't sprout a cucumber. It's a law of nature. And so it is with your thoughts. You can't expect harmony in your life and health in your body if you fill your mind with toxic thoughts.

Picture a vial that is filled with toxic poisons. At the base of the vial is a closed valve. If opened, the valve empties into an IV tube that is inserted into your bloodstream. I am absolutely certain that you would check that valve many times throughout the day, making sure that none of the poison would enter your body. Do you realize that negative thoughts and emotions, such as unresolved anger, hatred, bitterness, jealousy and revenge, are means of opening that valve, allowing that toxic poison to go into your system? Do you also realize that positive thoughts and emotions, such as love, forgiveness and acceptance, are means of locking that valve in the closed position forever, causing you to live a healthier and more peaceful life?

Many times people go through life like ships at sea. Sails open, they go whichever way the wind blows. They are not in control. But when you realize that you have a choice in how negative thoughts affect you, it's like putting a rudder in your hand so that when the wind blows, you can tack into the wind and use it to get to your destination. It puts *you* in control, not the thought.

In many cases, physical symptoms are merely the result of negative, angry, fearful or unhealthy thoughts. When we experience a headache, stomachache or other physical symptom, we need to stop and examine what thought process might be causing this physical response.

About ten years ago, my daughter, Cathy, and her family endured one of those years besieged with problems. In a ten-month period they experienced two automobile accidents, as well as the death of her grandmother, her husband's father, two family friends and the family dog. Her father-in-law became ill in the first week of June and remained in the hospital for three months until his death. The doctors expected him to go at any time, so my daughter and her husband kept a constant vigil at his bedside, taking shifts so that her husband could go to work during the day and she could spend the nights with their two small children, ages eight and four.

It was emotionally draining for them, and as they returned home from their fourth funeral that year, her husband said he didn't think he could take much more. But within six weeks, they experienced another setback, a house fire that gutted their home. They moved in with us while their home was being rebuilt.

During that time, Cathy's eight-year-old son, Ryan, began experiencing severe stomach pains. He would be lying in bed and suddenly double over, crying pitifully, because it hurt him so bad. When school started again, he began to call home because he felt nauseous. They took him to the doctor, hoping to find out what was causing the pain. The doctor ran a whole barrage of tests—blood workup, stool specimens, urine tests, even an upper GI to check for an intestinal blockage. When all was said and done, the doctor said she could not find anything medically wrong with him and she believed the pain was psychologically induced, due to the traumas he had experienced over the past year.

I began relaxation sessions with him and he soon realized that the pain seemed to come when he was worried about something. Things like returning home after the repairs were done or going away on vacation filled him with worry. Even a pleasurable experience such as going to the beach made him fearful to be away from home. He also learned that he had control over it. He learned to recognize the pain and notice what he was thinking at the moment it started. With this knowledge, he was able to relax and control the situation and the pain soon subsided.

Not long after that, their home was finished. When they were ready to return home, Ryan became nervous about leaving. I brought him into my office and asked him how he felt. He said, "Grandpa, I'm kinda scared. I don't feel good about going back to my room." I looked around my office and asked, "Well, how do you feel about this room?" "Oh, I like it a lot, Grandpa. I feel good here." "Well, do you know why? It has a good atmosphere. Do you know what that is?

It's the things around you. You can create a good atmosphere in your new room, too, by putting things around you that make you feel good, things that make you comfortable. If you could have one thing in this office that would make you feel comfortable, what would it be?" He looked around the room and said, "That picture." It was a Norman Rockwell print called *Outward Bound*. "Then take it. It's yours. That will be the beginning of *your* nice atmosphere." To this day, he has not suffered with the pain again, and *Outward Bound* still hangs above his bed.

His story is a perfect example of how our physical body responds to our thought process. When our thoughts are negative, we go into a self-destructive mode. Many times the symptoms we experience, such as tightness in our neck or shoulders, knots in our stomach, headaches, that feeling of pressure, are ways of our physical body telling us that we need to make a correction or change in something we are doing or thinking. It's like a warning signal going off. When you experience these negative responses in your body, you need to stop and ask yourself, "What am I thinking?"

It reminds me of a trip my wife and I took to the Ozark Mountains. We were really excited about this trip because we had been planning it for a long time. We even bought a new car. It was a Chrysler New Yorker and it was all computerized. We had just driven high up in the mountains when this cute little bell sounded and on the computer screen a nice little amber light lit up that read "BRAKES." Immediately my wife said, "You better stop as soon as we can and have the brakes checked." I tested the brakes and they seemed to work fine. I assumed it was a short circuit in the computer system, and since the car was running well and seemed to be working, I continued driving it with that nice little amber light on all that day in the mountains. The next day, the brakes began to grind and in a short time they sounded terrible. Finally, when I took my car to a garage in Hot Springs, Arkansas, I was informed that the brakes had worn the metal drum down so much that it was going to be a major job to do the repairs. It cost me $285.

If I had taken care of the problem when the light first came on, it would only have cost me about $30 or $40. But because I waited so long, it kept getting worse and required much more work to repair the brakes.

Now, I couldn't blame the car. I couldn't blame the mechanic. I couldn't blame the light. And I couldn't blame God. I tried to blame my wife, but she said, "I told you so!" (Don't you just love it when they tell you "I told you so!")

If I had read the owner's manual to see what the light was all about, I would have been aware that it was a warning of things to come. It would have saved me a great deal of money and "I told you so's." It was an expensive lesson, but a good one.

Many people take the same approach to sickness. It's so much easier to take a pill for a headache than to stop and see what is causing the headache. Find the cause and eliminate it, and the symptoms will heal themselves.

I remember a story that Dr. Art Winkler used to tell that illustrates the way many people try to solve a problem. The co-pilot of a large airliner approached the pilot and said, "Bill, I just saw the red warning light under the landing gear flashing on and off." "What did you do?" asked the pilot. "I unscrewed the light bulb." Many times we'd rather avoid the problem than make the effort to find out what caused it.

It is claimed that up to 70 million people in the United States have diseases and disorders of the digestive tract.

Many doctors say that stress can often be the cause of such problems.

I've worked with many people suffering with stomach ulcers who experienced relief after they learned to control their thought process. Although it is now believed that ulcers are caused by bacteria and not stress, I believe that stress can weaken the immune system, allowing these bacteria to flourish. It's been said that ulcers aren't caused by what you eat, they're caused by what's eating you!

I want you to understand that I'm not knocking doctors or medication. I believe that when you marry good medicine with positive thoughts and attitudes, you strengthen your body's natural healing process and increase your overall well-being.

Scientists are becoming more aware of the mind–body connection. They can detect chemical changes in the body due to thoughts. For example, people stressed out about a work deadline may have difficulty sleeping. This is evidence of altered neurotransmitters.

Negative thoughts and attitudes can weaken the immune system and slow down or stop the healing process. In December 1997, at the International Conference on the Psychology of Health, Immunity and Disease, a speaker shared with us some research involving the mind–body connection. The researchers had one group of people watch a violent movie. Blood samples were then taken from each person in the group, and their immune systems registered very low.

The next day, the same group watched a film about Mother Teresa ministering to the poor in Calcutta. Again, blood samples were taken after watching the film, and this time their immune systems registered extremely high. Their thoughts, their mental process, had a direct effect on their body—in this case, their immune system.

This connection between the mind, body and spirit is not just a modern-day theory. Ancient people realized this connection, which is evident in their writings. In the Bible, Romans 12:2 states, "Do not conform to this world but be transformed by the renewal of your mind." An ancient Chinese proverb reads, "The mind is the emperor of the body." And the Hindu Bhagavad-Gita (about 400 B.C.) says, "A man must elevate himself by his own mind, not degrade himself. The mind is the friend of the conditioned soul, and his enemy as well."

Just think about the statement "Do not conform to this world but be transformed by the renewal of your mind." How can you live in this world and not conform to it? It's a world bombarded by negativity, hatred, jealousy and greed. The only way to not allow these things to affect you is to function on a higher level of consciousness. You must use your awareness shield and not allow these negative things to penetrate and control you, and you must change the way you perceive things. By doing this you will not conform to the world, but rise above it. You will be in the world but not of the world. By this renewal of the mind, you can be transformed. Webster's definition of "transform" is "to change, to transfigure; to change into another form." It's a metamorphosis, like the caterpillar into the butterfly. It's no mere change in appearance. Biology tells us that it is a complete change. The tissues of the caterpillar literally dissolve and are reformed into a new creature. Isn't it beautiful? If God created such a miraculous ability in insects, don't you think He would create the same ability for change within us, His children?

You can be transformed by the renewal of your mind. That means that you can change whatever you want to change just by renewing this thought process, causing you to feel better not only physically but also mentally, emotionally and spiritually.

Hopefully, you now have a better understanding of the immense power of a thought. Remember, "*As a man thinketh, so shall he be.*"

Chapter 5

Hypnosis

Hypnosis is a highly misunderstood practice. When you ask most people what they think hypnosis is, their answer strongly resembles the images seen in a late-night horror movie or a Las Vegas stage act. They have a vision of Bela Lugosi's eyes staring intently, forcing a person to do things against their will. Or they have the misconception that a hypnotist will put them in a sleeplike trance where they have no control and no memory of it later. Some religions go so far as to claim it is the work of the devil.

The word "hypnosis" is derived from the Greek word *hypnos,* which means sleep, although hypnosis is not a state of sleep. Hypnosis is in no way a new practice. Stone carvings of sleep temples have been found dating back as far as 1000 B.C. In these temples, high priests put worshippers to "sleep." The worshippers were then given the suggestion that while they slept, some god or entity would come to them and they would be healed—and they usually were. Sleep temples became very popular with the Greeks and Romans from 400 to 100 B.C.

Hypnotic techniques continued to be used throughout the centuries. One of the most famous practitioners of these techniques was an Austrian physician, Dr. Franz Anton Mesmer, in the late 1700s. Modern hypnosis is believed to have begun with him. Mesmer believed that people had a magnetic field that, if disturbed, would cause illness. He called this "animal magnetism." He believed that placing metal plates around the body would create healing. His practices became very popular, especially with the French nobility. Many came to him to be "mesmerized." Mesmer was truly a master of suggestion.

The first physician to study Mesmer's work seriously was a Scotsman by the name of James Braid. Dr. Braid was the first to introduce the term "hypnosis." In the mid-1800s, Braid and two other physicians, Dr. James Esdaile and Dr. John Elliotson, used hypnosis in their practices in England. They performed many surgeries using only hypnosis as anesthesia. The mortality rate for major surgery at that time was about 50 percent. But in the 161 operations done by Dr. Esdaile, using hypnotic techniques and suggestions, mortality dropped to only 5 percent, with none of the fatalities being an immediate outcome of surgery. Dr. Esdaile considered hypnosis a natural God-given method of healing.

In 1847, the Roman Catholic Church issued a decree that stated, in part, "Having removed all misconceptions, ... the use of hypnosis is indeed merely an act of making use of physical media, and is not morally forbidden, provided that it does not tend towards an illicit end."

During World War II and the Korean War, hypnosis was used in the treatment of battle fatigue and for pain control.

Now, in the twenty-first century, hypnosis is more widely used by those in the healing professions, such as doctors, dentists, psychologists, chaplains, pastors and social workers. There is even a hypnotherapy organization, the National Association of Clergy Hypnotherapists, exclusively for members of the clergy.

But what exactly is hypnosis? Someone once asked Thomas Edison, "What is electricity?" To which he replied, "Electricity is—use it!" It's not necessary to know how electricity works, to turn on a light bulb. The same is true for hypnosis. But I want you to understand what hypnosis is and isn't.

Hypnosis is nothing other than an altered state of consciousness in which a person is guided with suggestions. Let me explain to you a little bit about the different states of consciousness, so that you have a better understanding of how this takes place. There are four primary brain-wave patterns, beta, alpha, theta and delta, which determine our state of consciousness. The beta state is the one in which we are fully conscious and aware. It is the one in which we spend the majority of our waking time. In the alpha state, brain activity slows; people experience deep relaxation and heightened creativity. This state produces hypnosis or deep meditation. We slip in and out of the alpha state many times throughout the day. In this state, we are alert but feel detached. In the theta state, brain activity slows even more. It is the state we experience just before we fall asleep and just before we wake. The delta state is the deep-sleep state.

We hypnotize ourselves every day. We move into these alpha, theta and delta states without any conscious effort. Let me give you some forms of this self-hypnosis or these altered states of consciousness. At night when you go to bed, for the purpose of going to sleep, you put your head on the pillow and close your eyes. You begin moving into an altered state of consciousness. You may be in that state for a minute or twenty minutes or even an hour before you move into a natural state of sleep, which is the delta state.

When you are hypnotized, you are not unconscious but within one of these altered states of consciousness. When you are in an altered state, the subconscious mind is in charge. The conscious mind is still there, but narrowed down to the point that the subconscious mind takes over.

You must understand that all of hypnosis is self-hypnosis. The only way you can be hypnotized is if you are willing to be. The hypnotherapist does not take control over you. You are in control at all times. When you're in a hypnotic state, no matter how deep, and given a suggestion that would be against your will, morality or religious beliefs, you would do one of two things. You would either reject the suggestion and let it go or come completely out of the hypnotic state and challenge the hypnotherapist. The hypnotherapist cannot force you to do anything against your will. Remember, as I mentioned before, your free will is one of the most powerful things you have.

Unfortunately, the only concept of hypnosis that most people have is what they see on the stage. I've had clients who did not understand why people would act silly on stage if the hypnotist did not force them to do it. I try to explain it to them in this way: People who attend this type of show are there for enjoyment purposes. When the hypnotist asks for volunteers, people who raise their hand are already agreeing to follow the hypnotist's suggestions. They are going up there to have a good time. If the hypnotist says, "When I count to three, you will bark like a dog," and everyone starts barking, would you be the only one who didn't? No, because then you would be the odd one. But when it's all over, their excuse for acting silly is that the hypnotist *made* them do it. At one of my seminars, a woman said, "I still believe you could be made to do something you didn't want to do." So I said, "Okay, would you come up here for a moment?" She did. I then asked her to sit down in a chair, so she sat down. I asked her to take a deep breath and she did. I then asked her to close her eyes and she closed her eyes. I then asked her to raise her right arm out in front of her and she raised her arm. Next, I asked her to take another deep breath, which she did. I asked her to place her left hand on her left knee and she complied. Then I asked her to take her right hand and place it on her right knee, which she did. I then asked her to get out of her chair and go stand on her head in the front of the room. She opened her eyes and said, "Pardon me?" I said, "Wait a minute. You followed eight previous suggestions. Why didn't you follow that one? Because it was against your will." Stage hypnosis is not the same as clinical hypnosis, but unfortunately it is the only form most people are familiar with.

There are many other forms of self-hypnosis that you may not even be aware of, though I'm sure you've experienced them. Have you ever been driving your car, just staring ahead of you, and suddenly realized you passed your exit? You were driving along and, without realizing it, moved into an altered state of consciousness. Suddenly, you jumped back into a fully conscious state and realized that you missed your exit entirely. Truck drivers call this "road hypnosis." It's a natural phenomenon. Sometimes you may drive somewhere and realize that you don't even remember how you got there. Your conscious mind was focused on something else.

Daydreaming is another form of self-hypnosis. Have you ever just stared at something and suddenly realized that someone had been calling your name and you didn't even hear it? That's an altered state of consciousness. The only danger of being in an altered state is not being aware of what you may be feeding directly into your subconscious mind. If, while staring off into space, you begin feeding yourself negative information such as "I don't know what's wrong with me; I can't seem to do anything right" or "I'm not happy" or "Life is miserable" or "I feel horrible," these things are going directly into the subconscious mind because the conscious is narrowed down to a point that it is not rationalizing or contradicting these thoughts. Remember, the subconscious mind accepts statements as truth. So what happens when you come out of the altered state? You begin to respond to the negative programming by feeling bad or depressed, and you don't even realize why.

Have you ever just sat staring at a fire in the fireplace? Soon your mind is very peaceful, your eyelids feel heavy, and thoughts are just flowing in and out; you're not focusing on any one thing in particular. Or maybe while reading a book, you became so engrossed in it that you thought you were reading for only a few minutes when actually an hour had passed. These are also altered states of consciousness.

Some people say, "Oh, I can't be hypnotized!" But without realizing it, they experience these forms of self-hypnosis on a daily basis. It's a natural phenomenon. Your mind already knows how to do it.

As I stated previously, I use hypnosis a little differently than other hypnotherapists. Because I know firsthand the importance of the mind–body–spirit connection, I work with a person's own spirituality to help them achieve their desired goal. I believe that when a person is in the hypnotic state, that altered state of consciousness, they are more in tune with *God consciousness*. It's like a holy encounter that takes place. They are able to see things more clearly, from a more knowledgeable, more relaxed and more spiritual point of view. They are able to rise above the problems and fears that once consumed and controlled them. On that level, when their perceptions change, they become free from that problem, and even though the conditions and circumstances remain the same, they are no longer affected by it.

I have briefly explained a little of what hypnosis is and isn't to help you understand it better and remove any misconceptions you may have had about this beneficial tool.

Chapter 6

The Power of Suggestions

Does anyone have a suggestion?
If so, put it in the suggestion box.

The subconscious mind is like a suggestion box. Each day, it takes in hundreds of subtle suggestions, some positive, some negative, placed there by ourselves and others. Unfortunately, the greater number of these tend to be negative, and without the use of some type of filter, in this case your awareness shield, your mind can become cluttered with negative suggestions that can create an unwanted response.

We, as humans, are highly suggestible beings. We respond to suggestions, from others and from ourselves, hundreds of times each day. Let me give you an example: I want you to picture a lemon. Notice the bright yellow skin and the smooth texture. As you cut into it, some of the juice squirts out, and you smell the tangy aroma. Now imagine lifting it to your mouth. You can really smell the tartness now, and as you bite into it, you can feel that squeaky sensation of your teeth against the pulp. You begin to suck the lemon, and the sour juice fills your mouth. As you read this example and thought about the lemon, did you notice your mouth watering a little? If so, you're not alone. Most people, at the mere suggestion of biting into a lemon, will experience the physical response of increased saliva.

Now, recall the altered states of consciousness and how we drift in and out of these throughout the day, unaware that we are doing it. While in an altered state, we are more receptive to suggestions, whether they are good or bad. If we accept the suggestion, we respond to it. In this way, we are hypnotized and not even aware of what is happening. An example of this is when children are told to eat everything on their plate because there are starving children in the world and it's a sin to waste food. That's a powerful suggestion. It gives the children a feeling of guilt for not eating, as if devouring everything on their plate would have an impact on world hunger! When these children become adults, they still respond to that old suggestion. Even though they feel full halfway through the meal, they continue eating because they don't want to be wasteful. I know many mothers who eat the leftover food on their child's plate because they don't feel right about throwing it away. Have you ever been cleaning the kitchen after a meal and found a little bit of food left in the pot? It's not enough to save for another meal, but instead of throwing it out, you eat it even though you're not hungry, simply because you feel guilty about wasting good food. I ask my clients this question: What would you rather do? Scrape that food into the garbage can and never see it again, or eat it and carry it with you for the rest of your life?

As a child, did your mother or grandmother ever say, "Get out of the rain; you're going to get sick" or maybe "You're soaking wet; you're going to catch a cold"? Recently someone told me, "I got caught in the rain yesterday and got soaking wet. I just knew I was going to get a cold, and sure enough, when I woke up this morning my nose was blocked and I had a sore throat." "Wait a minute," I said. "Do you take baths or showers?" She responded indignantly, "Of course, every day!" "And when you do," I asked, "do you get wet?" "Yeah, sure." "Then how is it you don't get colds every day?"

Simply getting wet will not cause people to catch a cold. If they do, they were probably exposed to the cold virus days earlier, or perhaps, as in this case, it was a response to an old suggestion. Their subconscious had held on to that suggestion and, in the right situation, responded to it. Remember, they "just *knew*" they were going to catch a cold, and their mind met that expectation.

I had someone tell me, "It never fails. Every year, at the first sign of winter, I end up with a cold." It's as if the cold germ were sitting on their shoulder, waiting for the first sign of winter, to jump into their body and cause misery.

Doesn't it make you wonder how many things are actually genetic and how many are just powerful suggestions that have been passed down through the generations? "Anger runs in our family. My father had a really bad temper and so did his dad." "I'll always be fat because my parents were overweight." "My kids are just like me. I always had trouble in math and they do too."

It reminds me of the story of the young woman who got married. She wanted to cook a pot roast for her husband and she remembered her mother's recipe. Her mother had taught her as a child how to cook a roast. It was always tender and delicious. So she used a cast iron pot, just like her mother. She seasoned it with pepper, garlic and onions, just like her mother. And then, before she placed the meat in the pot, she cut a piece off of each end, just the way her mother did. It came out wonderful, but she was curious about something and called her mother. "Mom, I made a roast just like you taught me, but there's something I don't understand. Why do you cut off the ends of the roast before you cook it?" "Well, honey, that's the way my mom taught me to do it. I think it makes it tender." Still curious, the girl called her grandmother. "Grandma, Mom taught me to cook a roast. She always cut the ends off the roast and she said that you did the same thing. I was just wondering why." "Well, child, I don't know why your mother did it, but I always cut the ends off because my pot was too small."

Simple suggestions have a way of altering our lives, and unfortunately, many in the health care profession do not realize the power of a suggestion. Without realizing it, some of these professionals give their patients negative suggestions that have adverse effects on their health and recovery. We put doctors on a pedestal. They are the authority, and if the doctor says it, it must be true. Just think about the well-meant negative suggestions that doctors sometimes give to patients: "There's no hope." "You have less than six months to live." "You have to face the facts and realize that nothing can be done." These suggestions can cause chemical reactions in the body that are harmful. Let's say I walk into any doctor's office and tell them, "I'm sorry. Your family has been in a terrible automobile accident and they were seriously injured." Even though this statement isn't true, they would experience panic, increased blood pressure and heart rate, and other physical and emotional changes that would have a negative effect on their body. If health care professionals would realize the importance of using the mind in conjunction with medicine, they could use a patient's suggestibility to aid in

f mind. If you're not using the
, it's like having your star quar-
st sitting on the sidelines.

y suggestible. Remember, their
not fully developed, so sugges-
by their subconscious, and as
d to them. You might say they
suggestions were given to them.
that when I help them break free
I am not so much hypnotizing
them!

story of a little girl who went to
ommy, am I an Indian?" "No,
sure I'm not an Indian?" "Yes,
other replied. "But I want to be
sted. "Why do you want to be an
Indian?" the mother asked. "Because I heard about these full-
blooded Indians and I want to be full-blooded."

A similar story someone shared with me is about a little
boy who excitedly told his mom that God made the world in
six days with only His left hand. She agreed that the Bible
says that God created the world in six days, but how did he
know that God only used His left hand? To which he declared, "Well, He must have because I heard Jesus was sitting
on His right hand."

These stories illustrate how children perceive things
differently. Remember, the subconscious mind accepts things
literally.

If you don't believe in the power of suggestion, just
look at the billions of dollars that are spent on advertising
each year. This is an industry that thrives on our suggestibility. Think of all the commercials and how they are designed

to suggest that you need a certain product to feel better about yourself or to be happy. What better way to influence you than to feed you these suggestions while you are in an altered state, such as blankly staring at a television screen? You are more receptive to them then.

That's one reason why it is dangerous for children to watch television unsupervised for hours at a time. Have you ever watched a child looking at television? They sit, slack-jawed, staring intently at the screen, absorbing *everything* they see. If you think that they're not in a deep altered state, try calling their name and see how long it takes them to answer you. Make it a point to sit down by yourself and watch a few hours of television, and be aware of how many incidents of violence, immorality, greed and negative behavior you see, even in animated cartoons and video games. These images and suggestions are going, unchecked, right into your child's subconscious and forming the basis for their belief system and personality. It's scary, isn't it?

It isn't only the children who are affected by these negative influences. We adults also absorb these violent images, and if we don't use control and reject these negative suggestions, we too will respond to them. Just look at the increased violence in our society. Road rage is a prime example of this. As parents, it is our responsibility to take control over these negative influences on our children. Limit their exposure to negative behavior. Let them watch television, but make sure it has educational value, or better yet, sit down as a family and watch programs or movies that teach morals or show positive values, such as respect and compassion. Then these will be the imprints and impressions that fill their subconscious and help them become more positive individuals.

I believe that it is important to start controlling these imprints and impressions even earlier, when the child is still in the womb. It has been documented that the fetus will respond to the emotions of the mother. If the mother watches a violent movie and feels fear, anxiety and anger, doesn't it make sense that the fetus will respond to these emotions also? It's a sobering thought when you realize the profound influence you have on the development of your children.

Negative suggestions don't always come from someone else. Sometimes we give ourselves subtle suggestions that can be harmful to us. After one of my seminars, a woman came up to me. She was bent over a walker and in a soft voice asked, pitifully, "Dr. Bauer, will you please pray for my arthritis?" I told her, "No ma'am." She was shocked at my reply and I said, "I will pray for you but let me explain something first. If you had a dollar bill you could go around and tell people, 'This is *my* dollar.' And you would be right. It would be yours. But if you gave it to me, it would no longer belong to you. You could no longer call it *my dollar* because you gave it to me. When you use the word *my*, you're claiming it as your own. If you don't want the illness, give it to God and quit saying *my arthritis*."

Later on during the reception, I saw her again. This time she was standing taller and moving around better. Smiling, she told my wife, "I feel so much better. I never realized what I'd been telling myself. I've decided to give it to God because I don't want it."

Using "my" before an illness is a subtle suggestion to yourself that the illness belongs to you—"my cancer," "my asthma," "my diabetes," and the list goes on. Quit claiming it and reject the suggestion.

Suggestions can also be nonverbal. Waving, motioning and pointing are all nonverbal suggestions. Another good example is the yawn. Next time you yawn, notice how many people around you will suddenly do the same thing. Nonverbal suggestions, as well as verbal ones, can cause chemical reactions within the body. If you don't believe this, notice what happens next time you're in traffic and someone flips you the finger. They don't have to say a word, but the simple motioning of the finger can cause the blood to rush to your face; you become agitated and soon you've opened up a Pandora's box of unwanted responses. Why? Because you accepted the suggestion and reacted to it. When someone flips me the finger, I turn it around. I answer with another nonverbal suggestion, the okay sign. I know they're just telling me I'm number one in their book, and I answer, that's okay by me.

Only a small percentage of what we communicate is done through actual words. The rest of our communication is done through eye contact, tone of voice, facial expression, body language, mannerisms and even telepathically. Haven't you ever been talking with someone and knew what they were going to say before they said it?

I know many people who wear their emotions on their sleeve. You can tell at a glance whether they're happy, sad, depressed or just plain aggravated; they don't have to say a word. These are all forms of nonverbal suggestions.

It is important for us to become aware of the suggestions, both verbal and nonverbal, that we give to other people. Are they negative or positive? And even more importantly, what suggestions are we giving to ourselves? Remember, our words have side effects, just like medication. Proverbs 16:24 says, "Pleasing words are a honeycomb, sweet to the taste and healing to the body." And Proverbs 12:25 states, "Anxiety in a man's heart depresses it, but a kindly word makes it glad."

I remember the story of a group of frogs that were traveling through the woods, when two of them fell into a deep pit. All the other frogs gathered around the pit. When they saw how deep it was, they told the two frogs that they were as good as dead. The two frogs ignored the comments and tried to jump up out of the pit with all of their might. The other frogs kept telling them to stop, that they were as good as dead.

Finally, one of the frogs in the pit took heed to what the other frogs were saying and gave up. He fell down and died.

The other frog continued to jump as hard as he could. Once again, the crowd of frogs yelled at him to stop the pain and just die. He jumped even harder and finally made it out.

When he got out, the other frogs said, "Didn't you hear us?" The frog explained to them that he was deaf. He thought they were encouraging him the entire time.

This story teaches two lessons. There is power of life and death in the tongue. An encouraging word to someone who is down can lift them up and help them make it through the day. A destructive word to someone who is down can be what it takes to kill them. So from this day forward, think before you speak and be careful of what other frogs tell you.

Many times we fail to realize that everything we do in this life has a ripple effect. Each thought and suggestion, whether positive or negative, each act, whether kind or unkind, each word that's uttered from our lips and each acted-out emotion, all have the same effect as dropping a tiny pebble into the smooth surface of a lake. The ripples from that action do not remain at the point of origin, but continually spread farther and farther outward. You may never know the true impact that a simple smile or kind word can have on others, but its effects can be far-reaching.

I found this poem years ago, and I've kept it as a reminder of the impact we have when we speak.

The Power of Words

Did you ever stop to consider the power of words?
Words make up suggestions and affirmations ...
By words a salesman sells his product and service,
By words the preacher proclaims the good news of faith.
By words, thoughts are implanted in the mind
and can be passed on from one person to another,
and from one generation to another.
There are words that make us laugh,
There are words that make us cry,
Words that bless, and words that condemn,
Words that are constructive,
and words that are destructive.
There are words that wound, and words that heal.
The most profound false statement ever
was the old saying
"Sticks and stones may break my bones,
but words will never hurt me."

—Author unknown

Let this be a reminder to you of the profound influence your words have on others.

Will you be an inspiration or a hindrance to their spirit?

*"Kind words can be short and easy to speak,
but their echoes are endless."*
—Mother Teresa

Chapter 7

Affirmations for Positive Programming

Remember, the subconscious mind can be compared to a highly sophisticated computer. But no matter how sophisticated it is, if it is programmed with the wrong information it won't perform the way it was designed to.

All day long, without realizing it, we are continually programming our subconscious mind by means of thoughts, suggestions, self-talk and affirmations.

The definition of "affirm" is "to declare or state, to make a statement and maintain it to be true." I believe that an affirmation is affirming something even before it happens.

Affirmations can be either beneficial or harmful to us. Just think of the negative affirmations we tell ourselves throughout the day: "I'm sick and tired," "I can't do anything right," "I can't lose weight," "Stupid me." The list is endless. Try to think of some of the negative affirmations you've been programming into your subconscious mind. Is that the reality you want to create for yourself?

The words "I am" are a powerful declaration. When you use this phrase, you are stating a fact very simply and emphatically. Anything that follows "I am" is going to become your reality. It's like a self-fulfilling prophecy. It is your perception of what is, and remember, what you perceive and believe will become your reality. "I am strong." "I am healthy." "I am happy." "I am going to do it."

No one seemed to understand this concept more than the world champion boxer Muhammad Ali. "I am the strongest." "I am the greatest."

To some he seemed conceited, but in actuality he was a master programmer. He consistently reinforced his belief system with these positive affirmations and he became what he believed, "the greatest champion in the world."

Affirmations are a way of building self-confidence and self-esteem. They are a wonderful way to block out and remove that old critical voice that says, "You can't do that."

Affirmations should be strong, positive statements about yourself that you believe or want to believe. You may not believe them the first time you say them. You may not even believe them the first several times you say them. But if you repeat them often enough, you will believe them.

You must be careful how you give yourself an affirmation. For example, "I no longer believe that I don't deserve to be successful." This is a mixed message the subconscious receives and takes as, "I don't deserve to be successful." Instead say, "I will be successful" or "I am successful."

When creating your own affirmations, it is also important to remember never to claim an illness or pain, for example, "My pain is gone" or "My body is healing my disease." When you use the word "my" in front of an illness, you are claiming it as yours. The subconscious mind wants to keep and protect what's yours. It also places the focus on the illness or disease. It is much the same as if I were to tell you not to think of a pink elephant. Immediately you would think of one because of the way the statement was presented to you. So be careful how you present affirmations to yourself and others.

On the following pages, you will find lists of affirmations that have been therapeutically designed to help you achieve your goals: affirmations for self-confidence and self-esteem, healing and good health, and weight reduction, as well as affirmations for children and a list of other good things to remember. Read all of the affirmations listed, and pick out some you like that have a special meaning for you. Repeat them often throughout the day. At night, when you go to bed, repeat those positive affirmations. When you first wake up in the morning, look in the mirror and say them to yourself.

Reading positive affirmations to your children is a good way to counteract many of the negative suggestions that are given to them throughout the day, at school, from peers, etc.

A positive affirmation is like a candle, and it will dispel the doubts and darkness. The more candles you light, the brighter the room becomes. The more positive affirmations you give yourself, the more that hope and faith will develop and project that affirmation into a reality.

Remember, we are creatures of habit. So the more you repeat the affirmations, the more they will become part of you, and your subconscious mind will make them into a reality.

When reading the affirmations to yourself, read in the terms "I" or "I am." If you are reading them to someone else, use the terms "you" or "you are."

Affirmations for Building Self-Confidence and Self-Esteem

I am special and unique.

I do not have to follow the crowd, because I am my own person.

I have many gifts and talents.

I have many skills and abilities.

I can do anything I put my mind to.

My determination to achieve my goals continues to grow stronger.

I am a worthwhile person because I was created in the image and likeness of God.

I am important.

I am a worthwhile person and God has a plan for me.

I am beautiful, inside and out.

I love myself because God loves me.

I am capable of changing.

I am a good person.

I am loved because I deserve love. It's my birthright.

I will practice being good to myself.

It's okay if I'm not perfect.

I accept myself as I am.

I like who I am, even though I don't always like what I do. I am human and ask God for forgiveness.

I have many good qualities to offer.

It's okay to make a mistake, because I will succeed.

I deserve to be happy.

I don't need others to approve of me, for me to approve of myself.

I am more calm and relaxed during my daily life.

I am more alert.

I feel more refreshed.

I am more composed.

I am more tranquil.

I am more at peace within.

I am more peaceful and calm in every situation.

At all times, I handle any situation in a calm and peaceful manner.

I am more effective and efficient in my work.

My confidence is increasing.

I am learning to be more in tune with my mind, body and spirit.

I am developing a more relaxed attitude.

I am more calm and relaxed, and that helps me think more clearly.

I have decided to think only good and happy thoughts about myself.

My life is becoming more enjoyable.

My feelings of happiness are increasing.

My day-to-day living is more pleasurable.

I am rapidly becoming the person I always wanted to be.

I am self-sufficient.

I am healthy.

I am acceptable.

I am capable.

I am strong.

I have outstanding capabilities.

I have outstanding potential.

I have the mental and physical abilities to be an outstanding success.

I am developing more confidence in myself each day.

The kingdom of God is within me.

I have the ability to do everything I want to do, as well as everything I need to do.

I have many reasons to have complete confidence in myself.

I have the ability to set goals that I want to achieve.

I have the ability to perform the action required to achieve my goals.

I have the ability to be an outstanding success.

103

I am continuing to develop greater confidence
in myself.

I advance, progress and prosper in everything I do.

I have a greater sense of personal well-being.

I feel good about myself and the good things that
I'm doing.

I enjoy life more each day.

My happiness keeps increasing.

I am more enthusiastic and more optimistic
each day.

I see life as a wonderful experience with great
opportunities.

I continue improving.

I am more able to depend upon myself.

I have increased confidence in my own judgment.

I have confidence in my own opinion.

It's easy for me to express my own point of view.

My self-confidence, self-reliance, self-acceptance
and self-esteem keep growing stronger.

I continue to be successful in everything I do.

My subconscious mind is accepting all of the affirmations and making them true.

My life keeps becoming more joyful, more productive, more useful, healthier and happier.

My spiritual awareness keeps increasing.

The right path to take and the right decision to make keep becoming more clear and understandable.

My love and understanding continue to grow.

I am a good person.

I am a loving person.

I am a child of God.

My mind is at peace.

I can achieve anything I make up my mind to do, and I've made up my mind to be the person I really want to be.

I can and will be transformed by the renewal of my mind.

Affirmations for Healing and Good Health

I am peaceful and serene.

My subconscious mind is sending out healing to every part of my body.

God created my body to be healthy.

I will allow all the natural healing processes that God gave me to function perfectly.

I realize I can be transformed by the renewal of my mind.

I am renewing my mind with good thoughts.

The kingdom of God is within me.

Love and forgiveness will clear the path to healing.

Forgiveness will heal all emotional wounds.

Forgiveness and love will heal all things.

Forgiveness and love will heal my body, give peace to my mind and set my spirit free.

I deserve to be healthy and strong.

I thank God for today, and I live and enjoy today in its fullest.

I choose to think only happy thoughts.

I expect good things to happen in my life.

My immune system is getting stronger each day and producing good health in my body.

All of the processes of my body are functioning perfectly.

My firm desire is to be healthy and strong.

A relaxed mind and body promote healing.

It's okay for me to take time to develop a healthy body.

I take the time for myself to exercise my body regularly.

I am my body's keeper.

I take care of my body and I always treat my body well.

My body is the only vehicle I have to experience life with.

I want to experience the rest of my life in a strong, healthy body.

It is God's will for me to be healthy.

Faith, expectation and determination can change my life and my health.

My body was created by God to heal itself from within.

With God all things are possible.

Affirmations for Reducing Your Body

It is important not to use the word "lose" when refer-ring to weight reduction. For example, "I will lose weight." None of us like to lose anything, and if we do lose it, we normally want to find it again. The subconscious mind accepts things literally, and in this context it will help you find what you lost, the weight.

I highly recommend that you take some of the affirma-tions that are most meaningful to you and repeat them often throughout the day.

**I have made a decision to reduce my body
to a level that is pleasing to me.**

I look forward to being slim.

I am reducing my body in a safe way.

I eat only when I am hungry.

**I am developing my own technique of therapy
for reducing my body.**

I deserve to be slender.

My body was not created by God to be overweight.

**I feel good, now that I have made a decision to
reduce my body.**

I feel good about myself and what I'm doing.

My stomach is gradually shrinking.

I eat just the right amount of food to keep
my body nourished and healthy.

I enjoy choosing healthy and nutritious foods
because I know it is what my body needs.

It's normal for me to eat only when my body
needs food.

I am my body's keeper.

Reducing my body to a slim, trim size is easy
for me.

When my stomach muscles are being stretched,
it will send a signal to my mind to stop eating.

My body processes are functioning properly.

My digestive system is functioning properly.

My metabolism is functioning properly.

Water flushes out excess fat and cellulite
from my body.

I enjoy drinking water.

Water is cooling and soothing.

I am in control.

It's safe for me to be attractive.

It's safe for me to be slim.

I will always think of myself with good thoughts.

The more I love and take care of my body,
the healthier it becomes.

I am enthusiastic about reducing my body.

I visualize my body slim and trim.

It's okay if it takes some time to develop a slender
body, because it's permanent.

I eat only when I am hungry and not according to
a set time.

I deserve to take the time to exercise my body
regularly.

Walking is a safe and enjoyable exercise.

I have outstanding capabilities and I am using
those capabilities to reduce my body.

I take small bites and enjoy eating slowly.

**I am healthy, happy, thin, and full of energy
and vitality.**

**My health continues improving more and more
each day.**

**I will be an inspiration to others by what
I have achieved.**

Nothing tastes as good as slim feels.

Take a few moments each night, before you go to bed,
to close your eyes and visualize your body exactly the way
you want it to be, slender and healthy.

Positive Affirmations for Children

The following affirmations can be read to your child, just as he or she is falling asleep. You can read them as you would a story. Be sure to read them just as they are written. Speak in a whisper loud enough to be heard, but soft enough to allow the child to sleep. Affirmations can be read every night if desired, and then once or twice a week whenever needed.

You are a wonderful person.

You continue to feel better about yourself each day because God created you in a special way.

You are a very good friend.

You make friends easily because people naturally like you.

You are healthy and happy.

You are very intelligent.

You are very loving and kind to yourself and others.

You are a very loving person.

It's easy for people to like you.

113

Learning is fun.

You learn very easily and enjoy learning.

You have a good memory.

You enjoy school more and more each day.

**You love yourself and respect yourself,
so you take care of yourself.**

You are a child of God.

You are a wonderful and loving person.

You have pleasant and enjoyable dreams each night.

You are safe and protected.

I (We) love you more and more each day.

You are loved and respected.

At one of the seminars I conducted for a nursing group, I handed out a copy of these affirmations. I received a telephone call the next day from one of the nurses in the group. "I just wanted to call and tell you what an impact those affirmations had on my eight-year-old son," she said. "I read them to him last night, and this morning he woke up, made his bed and when he came downstairs he asked me if I could read him that 'story' again tonight. 'You know, Mom, the one that you read me last night that makes me feel good.'"

114

Good Things to Remember

The following are positive life guidelines that can be used as affirmations. Read through the list and choose the ones that have special meaning to you. Then repeat them to yourself often.

A peaceful mind gives health to the body.

Affirm it, visualize it, believe it, and it will actualize itself.

A peaceful mind generates power.

Alter your life by altering your attitude.

Believe in yourself.

Always picture success, no matter how badly things seem to be going at the moment, and be thankful even on the grayest day.

Ask for the ability to do your best, and leave the results confidently to God.

Attitudes are more important than facts.

Be bold, and mighty forces will come to your aid.

Be optimistic!

Because we can cultivate a habit, we therefore have the power to create our own happiness.

Make a habit of being happy.

Do the best you can, and leave the rest to God.

Believe that God will always make a way where there is no way.

By practicing faith, all you have to remember are two words: "I believe."

By praying, you feel better, do better, sleep better and are better.

By talking of good results, you invoke the law of positive effects and good results occur.

Go to the Lord if you are weary, and He will give you rest.

Cultivate friendships with hopeful people.

Day by day, as you fill your mind with faith, there will ultimately be no room left for fear.

Do away with the negative!

Do not believe in defeat.

Do not build up obstacles in your imagination.

Faith can move mountains; doubt can create them.

Do something, even if it turns out wrong.

Doubt closes the power flow; faith opens it.

Expect the best, and with God's help, you will attain the best.

Expecting the best means that you put your heart into what you want to accomplish.

Faith is the one power that fear cannot stand.

For a better and more successful life, cast out those old, dead, unhealthy thoughts!

Get a correct mental attitude, remembering that the ease or difficulty of anything depends upon how you think about it.

Give strength to people, and they'll give affection to you.

Go out of your way to talk optimistically about everything.

God has placed in our minds all the potential powers and abilities we need for living in peace.

God will fill your mind with courage, with peace, and with calm assurance.

117

God will not give you any greater blessing than
you can believe in.

Have faith in God and faith in yourself.

How we think we feel has a definite effect on
how we actually feel physically.

I can do all things through Christ, who
strengthens me.

Empty your mind of negativity at least twice a day
and more often if necessary.

If God is for us, who can be against us?

If we have faith, nothing is impossible.

If you drop a prayer into the subconscious
at the moment of its greatest relaxation,
the prayer has a powerful effect.

If you think victory, you get victory.
If you think defeat, you get defeated.

As a man thinketh, so shall he be.

In the quiet, we become aware of God's presence.

Be still and know that I am God.

It's not worth it to spend a thousand dollars' worth of emotion on a five-cent irritation.

Joy itself possesses healing power.

Forgiveness sets you free.

Know the truth, and the truth will set you free.

Learn to be a practitioner in hope until you become an expert in faith.

Let not your heart be troubled, nor afraid.

You can be in the world, but not of it.

Neither age nor circumstance needs to deprive us of our happiness.

Nobody can be you as effectively as you can.

Our emotional life is profoundly regulated by our thought life.

Our physical condition is determined very largely by our emotional condition.

Peaceful thought images will work upon your mind as a healing medicine.

People are defeated in life not for lack of ability, but for lack of belief in themselves.

Practice being peaceful.

Practice being relaxed.

Practice believing that God is with you and in Him you have the power to handle anything.

Practice confidence and faith, and your fears and insecurities will soon have no power over you.

Pray a great deal and always let your prayer take the form of thanksgiving.

Pray for healing peace in your nervous system as well as in your soul.

Pray with the belief that sincere prayers can reach out and surround your loved ones.

Reduce tension by reducing your own pace. Slow down and smell the roses and enjoy the sunsets.

Remember you can change any habit with God's help.

Develop the habit of being happy.

Spend most of your prayers giving thanks.

Surround yourself with friends who think positive, faith-producing thoughts.

That which is greatly believed will come upon you.

The kingdom of God is within you.

The man who assumes success tends to already have success.

The mind can be quieted by first making the body quiet.

The more you pray for other people, the more good results will come back to you.

The secret of achievement is to hold a picture of a successful outcome in your mind.

The way to happiness is to keep your heart free from hate and your mind free from worry.

Things become better when you expect the best instead of the worst.

Think calmness, and your body will respond.

Think in terms of expectation, not doubt.

Think it, and you can be it.

Think success, and you are bound to be successful.

This is the day that the Lord has made. Be glad and rejoice in it.

Tranquility is one of the most beautiful of all English words. (Use it!)

Do all things in moderation.

We can talk ourselves into either negative or positive results.

Whatever you take into your mind can grow there.

A prayer sent out for another person
also brings rewards into your own life.
(What goes around comes around.)

Positive words have a profound suggestive power,
and there is healing in the mere saying of them.

You can create any condition by the power of thought.

Your mental attitude is your most important factor.

Your mind will stay in perfect peace if it stays
on God.

Chapter 8

The Fork in the Road

As with any journey, you've come to a fork in the road. In the previous chapters, you learned about the subconscious mind and how it functions, and about the influence your belief system has in shaping your destiny. You've learned about the importance of positive thoughts and the power of suggestions. And by now you should realize that you are the only one who can change your life, by changing your perceptions.

You've gained wisdom as your traveling companion. Proverbs 3:13-18 says, "Happy the man who finds wisdom, the man who gains understanding! For her profit is better than profit in silver, and better than gold is her revenue. She is more precious than corals, and none of your choice possessions can compare with her. Long life is in her right hand; in her left are riches and honor. Her ways are pleasant ways and all her paths are peace. She is a tree of life to those who grasp her and he is happy who holds her fast."

But as valuable as this knowledge is, it is useless unless it is followed by action. Without putting it into action, it remains nothing more than a good intention. And in the words of my old parish priest, "The road to hell is paved with good intentions."

Once you have the knowledge and your awareness shield in place, you will be able to recognize the negative influences around you and understand how they can influence your life. Only by action, by changing the way you perceive the situation and by *choosing* not to let it affect you, can you overcome the obstacles in your path.

In India, when elephants are trained, control is established while the elephant is very small. A chain is placed around the baby elephant's leg and attached to a three-foot iron stake that is driven into the ground. For several days the baby elephant pulls and tugs and strains against the stake and the chain, but he is too small to dislodge it. Soon he is convinced, by this experience, that the three-foot stake and chain have the power to bind him. He no longer attempts to pull free. Ten years later, when the elephant is fully grown, weighs thousands of pounds, and is capable of uprooting trees and pushing or pulling a loaded railway car, he can still be held by a three-foot stake! Yet, if that stake were as big around as a telephone pole and planted as deep, he could easily uproot it! How can the stake and chain hold the elephant? By control and conditioning.

It is much the same with us. Negative experiences and false imprints and impressions have gone into our subconscious mind and been accepted as truth. Many times these experiences and false beliefs control our way of life. We become like the elephant, totally bound by them. But through awareness and control of our thoughts and emotions, we literally break the chains that bind us!

We should never allow negative past experiences to affect the rest of our lives. Mark Twain once said, "A cat may sit on a hot stove once and it will never do it again. But neither will he sit on a cold stove."

So here you are, at the crossroads. You must make a decision. You can continue down the same road you've been on—responding to situations spontaneously, letting them affect you mentally, physically and spiritually, allowing negative things in the past to disrupt your future—or you can choose a different road. On this road, guided by wisdom and knowledge, you are in control of situations instead of being controlled by them, you are free from all the false beliefs of the past, and you are open to God's healing grace and willing to make the changes that will lead to a happier, more peaceful and more productive life than ever before. I can tell you from personal experience that the old road will eventually lead to self-destruction.

You have to be at a point in your life where you are willing to make a change. The greatest success I've experienced with clients who want to quit smoking, reduce their weight or overcome addictions or other problems, occurs when they reach a point in their life where they are tired of how their life is being affected and want to change it for the better. Even though they may not believe they can quit smoking or overcome that problem, they still can, because that false belief, put there by themselves or others, can be changed. But first, they must have the desire and determination to do it. One of my favorite stories that illustrates this point comes from the New Testament in Luke 18:35-43. As Jesus approached Jericho, a blind man was sitting by the side of a road, begging. Hearing a large crowd going by, the man asked what was happening. They told him, "Jesus of Nazareth is passing by." He began to shout, "Jesus, Son of David, have pity on me!" People around him began to tell him to be quiet, but he continued shouting, "Jesus, Son of David, have pity on me!" No matter how much he was told to keep quiet, he continued shouting all the louder. Jesus stopped and ordered that the blind man be brought to him. When he came near, Jesus asked him, "What do you want me to do for you?" "Master, I want to see." Jesus said, "Go, your faith has saved you." Immediately the man could see and he followed them, praising God.

The blind man had the desire to see; he even believed that Jesus could heal him. But it took something more. It took stepping out in faith, calling on Jesus and not letting anyone hinder him. It didn't matter how many people told him to give it up, not to bother Jesus and just be quiet, he was determined to get Jesus' attention. And this he did. There were probably many other people who wanted to be cured of their illnesses along that road. They had the desire. And I'm sure many of them believed Jesus could heal them. But they didn't take that extra leap of faith. They didn't call out to Jesus. Maybe they didn't call out because they were afraid of what others might think. Or maybe their faith wavered a little. Perhaps they did start to call out to him, but as soon as someone told them to stop, they gave up. Maybe it was just easier for them to sit there and let the opportunity pass them by. Because taking that leap of faith, that different road, isn't always easy.

Everything in this life has a price tag. Have you ever walked into a store and fallen in love with a dress or suit that you thought looked great on you? You really wanted it until you looked at the price tag. You decided it was just too much, but a few days later, you regretted not getting it and paying the price.

It's the same in all areas of your life. Some people, for example, may long for a lean, muscular body. Everyone has the same muscles as a champion bodybuilder. The only difference is that champion bodybuilders are willing to pay the price. They are not only determined, but also willing to spend hours in weight training, pushing themselves to the limit and enduring fatigue and sore muscles to achieve their goal.

Some people may have a beautiful voice and long for a singing career. The only difference between them and professional entertainers is that the ones who made it to the top took that extra leap of faith. They were willing to pay the price of leaving their comfort zone to push and have their demos heard. They were willing to face some rejection along the way and determined to make it.

What is the price tag on your goal? What will it require you to do, and are you willing to do whatever it takes to achieve that goal? You don't want to wake up a few years from now and regret not paying the price.

It reminds me of the man who was out of work. He wakes up in the morning and says, "I wish I had a job. God, please help me find one." He sits down and has a cup of coffee and eats breakfast. The kids go off to school and he says, "Lord, I don't know what I'm going to do. The bills have to be paid and we don't have any money left. God, please help me find a job." He sits down, watches television and worries about not having a job. He eats supper, and before he goes to bed he says, "Oh God, help me find a job." The next morning, he wakes up and says, "God, help me find a job." The man had faith. He even had the desire. But he didn't put it into action. God isn't going to show up on his doorstep, like Publishers Clearing House with balloons and a check. The man needed to take that leap of faith, step out and look for a job, and God would show him the way. In Matthew 7:7, Jesus says, "Ask and it will be given to you, seek and you shall find, knock and the door shall be open unto you." He didn't say where you had to seek or what doors to knock on, he simply said do it.

Just because we've learned what we should do, doesn't necessarily mean we do it. The way we react to situations comes from habit. It's the way we've programmed ourselves to respond. It takes a conscious effort to break the habits we've formed. It's not magic and it doesn't happen automatically. Like the blind man, you have to take that extra step.

You must remember that each choice you make in life will bring you either closer to the light or farther away from it, toward the dark. When you make the right choice, the good choice, it will change you for the better, and with each one, you bring more light into yourself. Each time thereafter, it becomes easier to make the right choice. But you must realize that the same is true for each bad choice. When you choose to act negatively, it takes you farther away from the light and leaves you a little emptier. The more empty you become, the easier it is to make more negative choices.

Many times throughout each day, you will find yourself at a fork in the road. You will be at that point where you know what you should do, but are you willing to make a change, no matter how difficult it may be? Will you follow the old path or the new one? When someone pulls out in front of you in traffic and gives you the finger, when a co-worker fails to do their task and it becomes your responsibility, when you find someone talking about you behind your back, are you going to respond from habit or are you going to take that extra step?

Next time someone flips you off, try flashing them your biggest smile and giving them the okay sign back. Notice how good it makes you feel. For one thing, you've totally confused them and they'll be wondering about you the rest of the day! More importantly, you've taken back the power you would have given them in the past. When you respond spontaneously, you give them power, the power to make you angry, hurt and upset. And who does it affect? Not them. They went about their business and never gave it another thought, but you, on the other hand, stewed about it all day. Proverbs 12:16 says it best: "A fool immediately shows his anger, but a shrewd man passes over an insult."

When something happens that upsets us, we have a tendency to dwell on that one thing until it literally consumes us. For example, let's say you had a favorite pen. This particular pen meant a lot to you because your children saved their money and bought it for you when they were small. It has a great deal of sentimental value, and every time you looked at it, it reminded you of their love and the sacrifice they made to get it. One day you lay it down in the bank, and when you turn around it's missing. You ask around, but no one has seen it. You begin to wonder about who could have taken it. Was it the teller? Did someone else just walk by and pick it up? Maybe it was the person behind you. You had only turned away for a couple of minutes. Why would someone want to do that? It doesn't mean anything to them; it's just a pen. It meant so much to you and now it's gone. You just can't trust anybody these days. They don't have any consideration for anyone's feelings. *Now stop.* Do you see the power you had given to the pen? By responding spontaneously, not stopping and really looking at the situation, you let your emotions run wild. Your hurt, anger and frustration kept building each time you went over what had happened. If you would, however, take the time and view the situation from another perspective, you become in control. Your pen is missing and although you may miss it, nothing else has changed. Your children still love you and the sacrifice they made when they were small has not diminished. Only the material object is gone. Your children's gift of love is now shared with someone else. Can you see the difference? *You* now have the power, not the pen.

Once you no longer react spontaneously, you begin to view life from a higher level of consciousness and your life will improve dramatically. That is not to say that you will never again feel anger, jealousy, fear, resentment, etc. These are normal human emotions. But now you can see them for what they are, simply feelings. You may still experience them, but you now know that they are merely human reactions and you can let them go. You don't have to nurse them or give them the power to take over your life. You will be amazed at the feeling of freedom that comes from letting go of these negative emotions.

But it requires determination on your part because it may not always be easy to let go. Remember, it's your choice. Is it better to be right or happy? Do you want to be bitter or better?

Your happiness and well-being rest in your own hands, so take the responsibility for it. No one or nothing else can make you happy; only you have control over that. And you must realize that you cannot make someone else happy either. You cannot control or change someone else's emotions. They must be willing to do so. If God does not take away a person's free will, how can you? When you have trouble remembering this, say the Serenity Prayer: "God, grant me the serenity to accept the things I cannot change, the courage to change those that I can and the wisdom to know the difference." The key factor is knowing the difference.

The things you've learned in the previous chapters have given you a protective shield, your awareness shield. Use it. It will help you decide the direction you want to travel. You can only move in two directions, either toward the light or toward the dark, and the choice is yours. Remember, it doesn't matter where you are along the road; it only matters that you're moving in the right direction. Each step, each choice, no matter how small it may seem, has the ability to alter your course and your destination.

Chapter 9

The Dream Stealers

On your journey toward the light, you've gained wisdom and discovered your protective shield, awareness. But there's something lurking in the shadows that you must learn to recognize and avoid, or else become its victim. *Beware of the dream stealer!*

If I were to ask you to describe a grave robber, you would probably get a mental picture of a sinister-looking person creeping around a cemetery at night, carrying a lantern in one hand and a shovel in the other. They lurk in the shadows waiting for the opportune moment to carry out their dirty work. But if I were to ask you to tell me what a *dream* robber looks like, it wouldn't be quite so easy.

We are easy prey for the dream stealers because they are masters of disguise. The dream stealer could be hiding behind the face of a well-meaning friend, a spouse, a loved one, a co-worker, or even behind the face of the person looking back at you in the mirror.

Have you ever been truly excited about something and felt fairly confident about doing it? You share the news with a friend, looking for a little reassurance, but what you get instead is a questioning look and a mountain of what-ifs. Suddenly, all of your excitement flies out the window, followed by your confidence. You begin to question yourself, and for some unknown reason, their opinion becomes more valuable than your own. You've just been *zapped* by a dream stealer!

Maybe the opportunity comes along to start a new job or open your own business. It's something you always wanted to do. You are filled with excitement at the prospect, but when you share the news with your spouse, he or she shakes their head and asks if you've really thought this out. Do you realize how hard it is getting started? how much time is involved? You probably won't make as much money, and what about benefits? You have a few years invested in your current job, and what if this doesn't work out? You may not have the best job, but it's steady. Suddenly, you begin to think your spouse is right and you thank your lucky stars that he or she was there to stop you from making a huge mistake. *Zap!* The dream stealer strikes again.

There's a story of an old man who lived by the side of the road and sold hot dogs. He was hard of hearing, so he had no radio. He also had trouble with his eyes, so he didn't read the newspaper. But he sold hot dogs. He put up signs along the highway telling how good they were. He stood on the side of the road and cried, "Buy a hot dog, mister?" and people bought. He increased his meat and bun orders. He bought a bigger stove to take care of his growing trade. He was happy selling hot dogs, and people enjoyed doing business with him. One day, his son came home from college to help him out. And then something happened. His son said, "Father, haven't you been listening to the radio? Haven't you been reading the newspaper? The situation overseas is terrible. The domestic situation is even worse. Maybe it's not a good idea to invest so much in the business." Whereupon the father thought, "Well, my son's been to college. He reads the newspaper, he listens to the radio, and he ought to know."

So the old man cut down on his meat and bun orders. He took down all of the signs on the highway and he no longer bothered to stand on the side of the road to sell his hot dogs. And his hot dog sales fell almost overnight. "You're right, son," the father said to the boy. "We are certainly in the middle of a great depression."

It isn't that these people intentionally set out to burst your bubble. They probably have your best interests at heart. And in their mind, they're just trying to make sure that you've thought everything out before making such a big decision. They feel it their duty to point out every pitfall possible. They mean well, but I wonder how many dreams were never achieved due to a well-meaning dream stealer.

In some instances in the Bible, Jesus said, "Your faith has healed you." And in others he said, "Be healed. Go forth and tell no one." Why would he say tell no one? Maybe because Jesus knew that their faith could be shaken and they would allow someone else to take away what they had received. Maybe the first thing they would have done was to run up to someone and say, "Hey, look, I've been cured!" And all it would have taken was for that someone to say, "How did this happen? Oh, that guy Jesus did this? Well, you know, he doesn't have the power to do that. I remember him as a kid. He used to play games with my son. There's nothing special about him. I bet it won't be long before the leprosy comes back. You know, there's no cure for it." And suddenly their faith would be gone, replaced by doubt.

Doubt is the dream stealer's weapon. Where there is doubt, there is no faith. What happens is that you allow the dream stealer to plant a few seeds of doubt, and then you nurture them until they are in full bloom. Unfortunately, it's not always others who do the planting for us.

My younger son, John, at age twenty-one, was filled with doubt about where his life was headed and felt that there had to be more to life than what he was doing. He had a decent job, but working and going to school part-time left little time for anything else. We sat down one evening and he told me that he was considering joining the Navy. He said, "Dad, I've always felt like I was standing in a crowd, watching the parade go by." It broke my heart to hear that he felt that way. But he made the decision to step out of the crowd, to try something different. As I told him, "Go ahead and do it. Nothing has to be permanent." It wasn't easy, but he did it. And today, he is a corpsman with the Naval Reserves, a fireman and an EMT at a local hospital. He's also married to a beautiful girl, Keisha, and has a precious daughter, Kelsie. He could have been his own dream stealer, but instead he decided to march in the parade of life.

I myself had always wanted to write this book. From the time I experienced my profound spiritual healing to the present, I had gained so much knowledge. My life had improved so dramatically that I wanted to share it with others. I was excited at the prospect of helping others and sharing what I had learned. But when I thought about actually sitting down, compiling years of research and organizing it, it seemed an overwhelming task. I just couldn't find the time. It was too much to fit in between sessions with clients, talks and seminars. Maybe I was biting off too much. *Zap!*

One day I realized that I had become my own dream stealer. I then became determined not to let my dream die and not to let all the information I wanted to share go with me to the grave. I decided to step out in faith; it didn't matter how long it took or what was involved, I would see it through to the finish.

The reason the dream stealers have been so powerful in your past is because you were unable to recognize them. But now you should be able to see them clearly through your awareness shield. Once you are able to recognize them, it is easier to avoid them and resist their subtle, negative influence. I can't stress to you enough the importance of staying focused on your dream and the goal you want to achieve. Like the little dog in Chapter 1, it is easy to get sidetracked, and when you lose focus is when you are most vulnerable to the dream stealer.

Many times on my own journey, I allowed the dream stealers to fill me with doubt that caused me to question myself and the techniques I used to help people. In the beginning of my hypnotherapy practice, I was confronted with critical comments on the techniques I used. Other professionals told me that I referred to Jesus and the Bible too much when working with clients. One even told me, "Louis, you're a professional. When people come to you, they don't want to hear all of this religious stuff." Although my clients experienced an extremely high success rate, I began to doubt myself. My journey of self-discovery began because of a profound spiritual experience, but I started to think maybe these other people were right. Maybe it was turning people away and I was losing people that I otherwise could have helped. So for a time I tried not to use spirituality when dealing with clients, but there was something missing and my success rate was not as high.

Not too long after that, I attended a weekend religious seminar, and on the first day, one of the speakers began putting down positive thinking. He said that no one could be helped by positive thinking and if you believed that just your mind could do all these wonderful things, you were wrong. This floored me! Even though it was against what I believed, the seeds of doubt were planted.

I was confused. I didn't even feel like I belonged in my own religion. Driving to the seminar the next morning, I looked up at the sky and said, "Lord, if there is something here for me, you're going to have to let me know what it is. I don't feel like I fit in anywhere. Where do I belong? If there is something here that you want me to learn, you're going to have to show me."

When I arrived at the seminar, a woman came up to me and asked where she could find a particular verse in the Bible. When I opened my Bible, it fell open to Corinthians. The verse I was looking for was not in this particular book, but I began to read it anyway:

"Although I am free in regard to all, I have made myself a slave to all so as to win over as many as possible. To the Jews, I became like a Jew, to win over the Jews. To those under the law, I became like one under the law, though I myself am not under the law, to win over those under the law. To those outside the law I became like one outside the law, though I am not outside God's law but within the law of Christ, to win over those outside the law. To the weak, I became weak. I have become all things to all, to save at least some. All this I do for the sake of the gospel, so that I, too, may have a share in it" (I Corinthians 9:19-23). I had re-

138

ceived my answer. The woman was still standing there waiting. I apologized and helped her find her verse, but I was beaming. I realized that I didn't have to fit a particular mold. I had to be open so that I could reach all people.

Even though I felt I had received the confirmation I needed, the dream stealers have a way of sneaking up on you. Not too long after that, I attended another religious seminar. When it was over, I approached a church leader in charge of speaking engagements because I felt compelled to share the story of my healing. He was excited about my doing a talk for them until I handed him my business card. Suddenly, the excitement left his face and he said, "Wait, you're a hypnotherapist?" When I said yes, his whole personality changed and he said, "Well, we'll call you if we need you." Instantly, I was flooded with doubt again and those feelings of "not belonging" began to resurface. Driving home from the seminar, I prayed to God to give me guidance. Suddenly, I remembered this particular scripture: "John said, 'Master, we saw someone casting out demons in your name and we tried to prevent him because he does not follow in our company.' Jesus said to him, 'Do not prevent him, for whoever is not against you is for you'" (Luke 9:49-50).

The next morning, a very dear friend of mine and a deacon in the Catholic Church, Joseph Richard, called me. He said, "Louie, I did Mass last night and I don't know if this is going to mean anything to you or not, but during Mass I felt the strong desire to call you up and tell you this: Don't let anyone intimidate you." I felt better, and less than six hours later I received another call from Father DeGrandis, a friend and charismatic priest. He said, "Louis, I was just thinking about you and your ministry and what you were doing. I know you are going to be persecuted by a lot of people, because so am I. But just keep doing it. You are fortunate because you can touch and help people of all faiths, whereas mostly only Catholics come to me. Just keep doing it." What a confirmation!

I had lost sight of my goal, to help others, and by doing so had become vulnerable to the dream stealers. I realize that I don't have to justify what I do anymore. I don't have to defend it. I don't have to explain it. I don't even have to know how it works. I just have to do it.

I found this picture in a Christian bookstore. It holds a deep personal meaning for me and helps keep me focused on my goal instead of the opinions of others.

Universal Designers

"Being in God's flock doesn't mean I have to look like the rest of the sheep. I just have to follow the Shepherd."

As it says in Luke 11:33, "No one who lights a lamp puts it under a bushel basket. Instead they place it on a lamp stand where it will give light to all in the house." I've learned that I don't have to change the way I help people just to conform to someone else's concept of the "right way." I just have to charge onward, lamp burning bright, and He will take care of the rest.

It is the same for you. Decide on the goal that you want to accomplish and then work for it. But do not set yourself up for defeat by simply saying, "I'll try to do it." Be determined to *do* it, to succeed. There's a line from the movie *Star Wars* that really brings this point home. Yoda, the Jedi master, tells Luke, "There is no 'try.' There is either 'do' or 'do not.'"

Thomas Edison once said, "I speak without exaggeration when I say I have constructed 3,000 different theories in connection with the electric light, yet in only two cases did my experiments prove the truth of my theory." Edison didn't say, "I think I'll try to invent the light bulb." He worked hard to achieve his goal and he was determined to succeed. How many of us would have been that persistent? Your dreams will never become reality without taking that leap of faith and then working to achieve your goal. Edison also said, "Genius is 1 percent inspiration and 99 percent perspiration."

Once you've decided on your goal, you must follow up with action. Oliver Wendell Holmes said it best: "To reach the port of heaven we must sail sometimes with the wind and sometimes against it. But we must sail, and not drift or lie at anchor." Do whatever you need to do to accomplish your goal, what you feel is right, and don't get caught up in the results. Don't let yourself get bogged down with worrying about how you will achieve it. There is an old saying, "Once you begin to knit, God will furnish the yarn."

Whenever you feel yourself losing your focus, I want you to remember this story. It's found in Matthew 15:22-32: "Then Jesus made the disciples get into the boat and precede him to the other side, while he dismissed the crowds. After doing so, he went up on the mountain by himself to pray. Meanwhile the boat, already a few miles offshore, was being tossed about by the waves, for the wind was against it. During the fourth watch of the night, he came toward them, walking on the sea. When the disciples saw him walking on the sea they were terrified. 'It is a ghost,' they said and they cried out in fear. At once Jesus spoke to them, 'Take courage, it is I; do not be afraid.' Peter said to him in reply, 'Lord, if it is you, command me to come to you on the water.' He said, 'Come.' Peter got out of the boat and began to walk on the water toward Jesus. But when he saw how strong the wind was he became frightened; and beginning to sink, he cried out, 'Lord, save me!' Immediately Jesus stretched out his hand and caught him and said to him, 'O you of little faith, why did you doubt?' After they got into the boat, the wind died down."

Can you imagine this scene taking place? The other disciples were frightened, and when Peter began to step out of the boat, can you imagine their reactions? They were probably saying things like, "What are you doing, Peter? Are you out of your mind? What if you step out of the boat and that's not really Jesus? You're going to drown." "What if you can't get back in the boat? You better be careful. The water's deep and you don't swim that well." "Look out for those waves. What if they pull you under?" "Wait, Peter, we all love Jesus, but don't go overboard for him." But Peter knew what he wanted to do. He even took that leap of faith, stepped out of the boat and began walking on the water. But

142

when he lost his focus and started paying attention to the things taking place around him, he began to doubt. And doubt can literally cause you to sink!

I recall a fight I once saw on television. While changing channels, I noticed a boxing match about to begin. As I am not a fan of the sport, I couldn't even tell you who the opponents were. What caught my attention, however, is the look on the face of each of these young men. Prior to the match each one's face was set in a hard, determined scowl, their eyes locked in a piercing stare, as if daring the other one to even breathe. They were evenly matched, pound for pound, inch for inch, and each one reeked with confidence. You could see that each one felt assured of winning the title. The fight began and each came out like a lightning bolt. The first round, each boxed equally well, and when they returned to their corners, you could see the confidence on each one's face. Halfway through the second round, however, something happened that changed the tide. One of the boxers suddenly hit the other with two powerful blows that caused him to hit the canvas. When the stunned boxer looked up, you could see the change in his face. Suddenly there was doubt where confidence had been. And I knew it was over. Just the same as I in the audience noticed the change, so did his opponent. The opponent became empowered by the other boxer's doubt. When the boxer got up from the canvas, his opponent began a barrage of blows that left him covering his face and backing up against the ropes. The weaker he got, the stronger his opponent became, as if his weakness literally breathed life into the other. When the boxer finally moved his gloves away from his face, the only thing you could see was confusion and dismay. Gone was the look of "I'm going to win," replaced by the look of "What if I don't win?" Within two rounds it was all over. The young boxer had as much to do with his own defeat as his opponent did.

If doubt is the dream stealer's weapon, then "what if" is certainly his calling card. "What if I fail?" "What if it doesn't work?" Have you been confronted by a "what if" that's preventing you from achieving your dream? Use your protective awareness shield and you'll become immune to it. You'll become aware of what is happening and you won't allow it to change your beliefs or steal your focus.

Let's look at it from a biblical standpoint. Luke 8:43-48 states, "And a woman afflicted with hemorrhages for many years, who was unable to be cured by anyone, came up behind him and touched the hem of his cloak. Immediately, the bleeding stopped. Jesus then asked, 'Who touched me?' While all were denying it, Peter said, 'Master, the crowds are pushing and pressing in upon you.' But Jesus said, 'Someone has touched me; for I know that the power has gone out from me.' When the woman realized that she had not escaped notice, she came forward, trembling. Falling down before him, she explained in the presence of all the people why she had touched him and how she had been healed immediately. He said to her, 'Daughter, your faith has saved you; go in peace.'"

I want you to try to imagine this scene. The crowd was tremendous. Picture Jesus right in the middle of New Year's Eve in Times Square, the crowd pushing in from all sides. Something tells the woman that if she could just touch this prophet, this Jesus, she would be healed. She pushes through the crowd, reaching out her arms, straining to reach him. Jesus is also trying to make his way through the crowd, heading in the other direction. But she continues to struggle anyway, trying to make her way through the dense throng of people, knowing that if she could just reach him, everything would be okay. Slowly, she makes her way through the crowd. She is close enough now, and with her arms outstretched, she takes one final lunge, but only her fingertips brush softly past his robe. Immediately, she feels the bleeding stop and she is elated. But suddenly, above the noise of the crowd, she hears Jesus asking, "Who touched me?" The disciples, who are being jostled around with Jesus, cannot understand why he is asking such a question. "Lord, look at this crowd. It could have been anyone that bumped into you." But Jesus insists, "No, Peter. Someone touched me, I know it. I felt the power go from me." The woman begins to tremble. Why does he keep asking who touched him? She is afraid now that Jesus might be upset, and she falls at his feet, saying, "Lord, it was I. But I've been so sick for so long and nothing eased my pain. I knew if I could just touch you, I would be healed and everything would be okay." Suddenly, the crowd seems to fade around them as Jesus smiles, reaches out his hand and gently helps her up. "It's all right, child. Your faith has healed you. Go in peace."

This woman could have allowed herself to get caught up in all kinds of what-ifs. "What if I go to see this Jesus, and he's not there?" "What if I can't get through this thick crowd?" Or the ultimate what-if, "What if I touch him and nothing happens?" She could very easily have allowed someone else to dissuade her. But she didn't, not the people in the crowd who kept telling her, "Stop pushing! There's no way to get through here," or her well-meaning friends who may have said, "Are you crazy? What if, while trying to reach him, you stumble and fall? You could get trampled underfoot!" With determination, she persisted and in the end was rewarded. She was healed. "Remember, child, your faith has healed you."

Try using a simple technique the next time you have a tendency to say "what if." Add the word "so" in front of it, so your question becomes "So what?": "So what if it doesn't work?" "So what if I fail?" The only true failure is in ceasing to attempt.

Don't look at setbacks as failures, look at them as lessons that you've learned to help you accomplish your goal. You should never be afraid of setbacks because through them, you gain knowledge.

Fear and doubt are the enemy of dreams. We are born with only two fears: the fear of falling and the fear of loud noises. All of our other fears are learned. As Franklin D. Roosevelt said, "We have nothing to fear but fear itself." Only by facing your fears can you overcome them. There's a saying I once heard and it stuck with me: "*Fear knocked on my door; faith got up and answered it and found nothing there.*" Faith can remove your fears and help you become the person you want to be. You can either live your fears or live your dreams, but you can't do both.

It is also important for you to be careful who you share your dreams with. Make sure that it's someone who is going to support you. "Do not give what is holy to dogs, or throw your pearls before swine, lest they trample them underfoot, and turn and tear you to pieces" (Matthew 7:6). It's a good idea to create for yourself a dream team, people who believe in your dream, people to help you brainstorm and to boost you after setbacks.

Some people will undermine their own self-worth by comparing themselves with others. You can't use someone else's life as a measuring guide for your own. I myself

146

admired my teacher and friend, the late Dr. Art Winkler. Not only was he knowledgeable in the field of hypnosis, but he was also a very compassionate and spiritual man. As a novice hypnotherapist, I admired him so much that I wanted to be just like him. The more I tried to be like him, however, the more inadequate I felt. I soon realized that I could never be Art Winkler. Trying to be someone else would only make me a shadow of the man. But using the things I learned from him and the gifts I received from God, I could be the best Louis Bauer I could be.

What makes each of us special is that we are all different, with different goals and dreams, gifts and talents. And each dream is important, no matter how insignificant it may seem to someone else.

There is a story of a young woman who always wanted to be a doctor. She went to school, completed her internship, and decided she wanted to help people, not just at a hospital in the States but in India. In India, she took care of the sick and homeless, bandaging their sores and tending to their needs. There were no facilities, no hot or cold running water, and food was scarce. She didn't even have a decent place to stay.

One day, one of her associates decided to take a trip to visit her. He spent the day with her as she took care of the poor in the most appalling conditions. That evening, as they were sitting down to a meager dinner by candlelight, he said to her, "I wouldn't do this for a million dollars." And she answered him, "Neither would I."

She wasn't there for the money. She was following her dream. It's okay if some people don't understand your dream, because it's yours and, like you, it's unique. Never set your goals by what other people deem important, because you are the only one who knows what is best for you. Don't allow someone else's opinion to decide the fate of your dreams. You can be a king in your own kingdom or a slave in another's. Keep your focus, keep your faith, and you will achieve whatever you set out to do.

"A wise man makes his own decisions, and an ignorant man follows public opinion."

—Chinese proverb

Chapter 10

Releasing the Spirit

I want you to imagine a tower, tall and imposing, with thick stone walls. At the top of this tower is a prison cell. It is dark within the cell and the only light coming in is from a small window covered with iron bars. Imprisoned in this cell is a child with shackles on each leg and arm. The child can climb to the window and see out, but the bars and chains restrain him from going any farther. The child looks out of the window with longing, for there before him is a green valley that seems to go on forever and a blue sky with no boundaries. He longs to be free, to soar high above the green fields, weightless and unburdened. He knows that something else exists beyond the horizon, but he can go no farther because he is bound. The child's name is *Spirit*.

The human trinity is made up of the mind, body and spirit, and if our spirit is in bondage, we cannot be truly whole. When we hold on to negative thoughts and emotions, such as depression, anger, hatred, bitterness, jealousy, resentment, fear, guilt, greed and revenge, we literally forge the chains that bind us.

149

Have you ever used a garden hose? When you turn the water on, it will normally shoot out a stream of water that goes far beyond the end of the hose. But sometimes you turn the water on, full blast, and nothing happens. The first thing you do is check for a kink that could be stopping the flow of water. If you flip the hose to undo the kink, you may create another one farther down. You may find several kinks, and the longer the hose remains in that kinked position, the harder it is to remove them and the more it will have a tendency to kink in the same place. Only by stretching the hose out completely can you remove all of the kinks, allowing the water to flow freely again.

We, as humans, can be compared to this simple garden hose. God's healing grace is like the water. The tap is always on, full blast. We, however, stop the flow of His grace by kinking the hose. Each time we experience a negative thought or emotion, we temporarily stop the flow. When we release the negative thoughts or emotions, it becomes free-flowing again. But when we hold on to the negative thought or emotion, we create a kink, and that one kink may create several others that prevent the flow of God's grace. The longer we hold on to these negative feelings, the harder it is to release them, but it can still be done. It is only when we remove the kinks and allow that grace to flow back into our lives that we experience true joy and freedom.

Have you ever thought, "There must be more to life than what I am experiencing now? What am I here for? Is this it? Is there nothing more to life?" If you have, you're not alone. We have all had these thoughts at one time or another. What you must realize is that when you have these feelings, your spirit is crying out to be released. Examine your life and try to discover any kinks that may be preventing you from experiencing God's grace. Is it an addiction? unresolved anger? thoughts of revenge? jealousy? doubt? self-hatred? guilt? Whatever it is, only you can release it and help your spirit soar beyond the horizon. Remember, whatever you hold on to in your mind will create your existence.

As Ramakrishna (1836-1886) said, "It is the mind that makes one wise or ignorant, bound or emancipated. One is whole because of his mind, one is wicked because of his mind, one is a sinner because of his mind, and it is the mind that makes one virtuous. So he whose mind is always fixed on God requires no other practices, devotion or spiritual exercises."

There are certain established laws that exist in the universe. One example is the law of gravity. If you drop an object, the force of gravity upon it will cause it to fall. Another example is the law of the echo. If you were to stand on a mountain and shout "I love you," the echo would repeat it and you would hear the words "I love you" again and again. But if you were to shout "I hate you," it too would be repeated and come back to you over and over again. Remember the old saying "What goes around, comes around"? It's much more than just a saying. In its own way, it too is an established law of the universe.

Negative energy attracts negative energy in the same way that positive energy attracts positive energy. If you put out anger, agitation, disgust or resentment, you will receive these things in return. Maybe not at that exact moment, but it will come back to you sooner or later, and it will permeate your entire existence. But if you give out love, compassion, forgiveness, understanding and patience, these things will also come back to you a hundredfold. Your life will be full and rewarding. I can assure you, you do reap what you sow.

When I suffered from depression, I was filled with anger, bitterness, resentment and hurt. Soon, I couldn't see or feel anything else. It wasn't that my life was truly the way I perceived it, but it became the existence I had created for myself. Letting go of negative emotions is a major step to releasing the spirit.

Letting Go of Anger

Anger is a negative energy that is running rampant in today's society. It is like a mental cancer that, if left untreated, will consume and destroy you. Anger will launch the body's natural fight or flight response, in preparation for danger. The body releases the stress hormones adrenaline and cortisol into the bloodstream. Heart rate and blood pressure rapidly increase, blood tends to clot more rapidly and the immune system is temporarily suppressed.

Just look around and you can see examples of its destructive influence everywhere—shouting matches become shooting matches, children become angry with fellow students so they bring a gun to school, cutting someone off in traffic has become grounds for murder. "Road rage" is increasing at such an alarming rate and becoming so severe that I wouldn't be surprised to see it classified as a mental illness! One study at the University of Michigan in Ann Arbor followed 2,110 middle-aged men and found that those who expressed their anger in explosive ways, such as yelling, screaming or slamming doors, were almost twice as likely to suffer from a stroke as those who were better able to control their emotions.

In the case of road rage, another thing to consider is the social modeling factor. What are your children learning by your example? Consider the way you drive. When your children begin driving, they will most likely mirror your responses.

In some aspects, however, anger can be good. I'm not referring to unresolved anger, which is destructive in nature, and I'm certainly not advocating flying into fits of rage. Anger can be a release of pent-up emotions, and once released, it can spur someone to action in a positive way. Take, for example, the organization MADD (Mothers Against Drunk Driving), which has had a major influence on the reduction of drunk drivers nationwide. This organization was founded by a group of concerned women, among them Candy Lightner, who lost her own daughter, Cari, in a drunk driving accident. As a parent myself, I can understand the immense anger she must have felt, but instead of nursing that anger inwardly or striking out in a destructive way, this woman used it to make a difference in the world.

The same could be said about a man I admire, John Walsh, host of the television show *America's Most Wanted*. He had every right to be angry about the abduction and murder of his son Adam, but instead of letting that anger destroy him, he used it to make a difference. His anger spurred him on to positive action in working with law enforcement to apprehend criminals and in working with parents of other missing children.

It is natural to feel anger from time to time, but the danger comes when you hold on to it, dwell on it and nurse it. The Greek philosopher Aristotle once said, "Anyone can become angry—that is easy. But to be angry with the right person, to the right degree, at the right time, for the right purpose and in the right way—that is not easy."

By using your protective awareness shield, you will become aware of the things that trigger anger in you. Once you are aware of the "triggers," you will be able to avoid or overcome them.

Here are some techniques that you may find useful in helping you to overcome anger and anxiety.

Deep Breathing Technique

When something triggers your anger, instead of responding spontaneously, try breathing deeply. Concentrate on your breathing, and as you inhale, say to yourself, "I'm breathing in peace and contentment." As you exhale, say, "As I breathe out, I'm releasing all anger and negativity." Do this a couple of times. You will notice, as you do so, that you feel better and you are able to let go of whatever it was that was bothering you. This is a great technique that you will find helpful in a variety of situations.

Rose-Colored Glasses Technique

There is another helpful technique I like to use; I call it the "rose-colored glasses" technique. Imagine that you're sitting on a park bench. It's a beautiful, sunny day and you're sitting there resting. Your eyes are closed and you're feeling warm and contented. Suddenly, you feel something tapping your leg. You try to ignore it, but you can't. As the tapping continues, you become angrier. How could anyone be so inconsiderate? Finally, you can't take it anymore. You open your eyes, ready to do battle, only to see a blind man sitting on the bench next to you, gently tapping his cane on your leg. What happened to your anger? It became diffused when you looked at the situation differently and your attitude changed.

It's similar to the story of a man riding on the bus. At one stop, another man boards the bus with three small children. He sits down a couple of seats away from the other gentleman, and as the bus continues its journey, the children run up and down the aisle. The first man becomes agitated. He wonders how anyone can have so little consideration for other people. The children become louder, and as one child runs past him, she steps on his foot. "What's wrong with this guy?" he thinks angrily. "Doesn't he have any control over these kids?" Just then, another child bumps past him and knocks over his briefcase. He just can't take it anymore. "Hey, man. What's the matter with you? Don't you see what your kids are doing?" The other man leans over and says softly, "No, I wasn't paying attention. We just came from the hospital. Their mother died and I was trying to figure out how to tell them." Suddenly, the entire situation is changed because the first man is seeing it from an entirely different perspective.

The next time someone does something that agitates you, I want you to imagine yourself putting on a pair of glasses with rose-colored lenses. These glasses will help diffuse negative emotions because they allow you to step back and view the situation from another perspective. These glasses will give you a new insight that helps you realize that people aren't intentionally doing things to upset you. You just don't know what is going on in their life at that moment that causes them to act the way they do. So the next time someone pulls out in front of you in traffic, take a deep breath, put on your "rose-colored glasses" and think. That person wasn't sitting there all day, just waiting for you to come along, so they could pull out in front of you. You just happened to be in the wrong place at the wrong time. Don't take it personally.

Conscious Intent Technique

This technique helps you to practice your self-control, and as in all things, the more you practice the better you become. There are certain situations, for each of us, that are like "hot spots." Whenever you're confronted with these situations, it's almost a sure bet that your anger will be triggered. When you use the conscious intent technique, you purposely place yourself in the hot-spot situation and control it by a conscious decision. For example, in the city where I live, there is a particular intersection that I recognize as a "hot spot." A few feet past a major intersection, two lanes of traffic merge into one and cross a railroad track. At the intersection, all cars in the right lane should turn right; however, most of the time the cars on the right will race across the intersection and try to cut into the left lane. This not only causes traffic to back up in the left lane, but increases the possibility of a collision as cars race to get into the proper lane. As this spot is on my way home, it used to trigger me on a daily basis. I would find myself speeding up and riding the bumper of the car in front of me so that no one would be able to cut in. Now I use this situation for spiritual growth instead of spiritual hindrance. Even though I can avoid this hot spot by taking a back street and crossing the tracks a block farther down the road, I will sometimes purposely take the trigger route with the conscious intent not to let it affect me. As I approach the intersection, I will purposely slow down to allow other drivers to cut in. As I do so, I tell myself that it really doesn't make a difference whether they cut in or not. Their actions will not affect me or change the way I feel. When you face a trigger situation with this conscious intent, there is no way for it to affect you negatively. The situation no longer controls you, you control it.

The above are just a few of the simple techniques that you can use to help diffuse stressful situations that would normally cause you to become angry and lose control.

Letting Go of Worry

Sometimes we prevent the inflow of God's graces in other ways, such as when we are consumed with worry. Worry not only distracts us from our goals, but robs us of precious time that could have been spent developing our creativity or nurturing the soul. Remember the dream stealer's calling card, "what if"? What-ifs have a way of multiplying rapidly until, before you know it, there's an insurmountable mountain standing in your way.

One of my clients received this poem in an e-mail and I wanted to share it with you.

A little, bitty worry
started early in the day.
By noon it seemed my worry
hovered, standing in my way.
The things and thoughts I should have had
got buried in my mind,

until my little worry turned
into the horrid kind.
By bedtime, I was frantic—
what to do, oh what to do?!
And then I couldn't go to sleep
for worrying—fretting, too.
By morning I was almost sick,
when suddenly soon,
my worry had been all worked out
before the toll of noon.
Then I looked back and saw my worry
just for what it was—
a thing that didn't happen,
as worry seldom does.

—Bonnie Daisy Nelson

You may not even realize how often you worry about little things. Try keeping a journal for just two days. Every time you become worried about something, no matter how small, jot it down. For example, "I'm running a little late for work. Worried about not making it on time." Or, "I'm a little worried about a test that my child is taking. She needs to make a good grade." Or "I'm worried about what others will think of me if I don't do this." Or "If I don't get this done, ____ will be upset." Be very conscious of it for just two days. You will be amazed at the staggering amount of time you spend worrying.

A dear friend, Marvin, told me about an old plaque that belonged to his grandfather. Even though many years have passed, its timeless message still has a profound impact on his life:

Of all our worries,
Great and small,
The greatest of them,
Don't happen at all.

I can tell you, from my experience with clients, that about 75 percent of the things we worry about never come to pass, and another 23 percent are out of our control. Only an extremely small percentage of the things we worry about actually take place and are under our control. But worrying about them doesn't make a difference in any case.

The following is a simple technique that I use with clients who have the tendency to worry and can't seem to let things go.

Glass Jar Technique

Picture a room in your home. On one of the walls, imagine a shelf. And on this shelf is a glass jar, similar to an old-time, glass pickle jar with a screw-down lid. Imagine yourself taking the jar off the shelf and unscrewing the lid. Whatever you are worried about at this time, put it in the jar. Perhaps you are worried about a few things; if so, place them all in the jar. Now imagine yourself screwing the lid down tightly on the jar and putting the jar back up on the shelf. Now you don't have to think about these things anymore because they're safe in the jar. You can go back and get them at any time you choose. But for now, leave them in the jar. You don't have to worry about them anymore. You're free from them and you can enjoy the rest of the day with peace of mind. After experiencing this peace of mind, you may decide to leave them in the jar and not be concerned with them anymore. Should you decide to take the jar down and open it, you may find that there isn't as much in it as you put there. You may even find the jar completely empty, and realize that the things you were concerned about were really unnecessary worries.

Several of my clients have found great success in relieving stress and anxiety when they use this technique.

Placing your concerns or worries in the jar helps you to see them for what they are and you no longer magnify them. You stop blowing them out of proportion. Developing the ability to place things in the jar help you to better understand how to put things in God's hands and let them go.

When you put something in God's hands, you have to leave it in His hands. Most of the time, people will put something in His hands only to snatch it right back by continuing to worry and fret about it. That's like telling God, "I don't believe that You will help me. I think I can do a better job myself." When you give something to God, have faith that He will take care of it, so you can let it go.

Letting go doesn't mean giving up control. It's realizing that there are some things that you can't control or change. And letting go of things doesn't mean that you don't care. It's simply realizing that you care enough to do your best, and that's all you can do. Notice I said "*your* best." You can't do it for someone else; that's not within your control. Letting go means accepting that you're only human. If you want to achieve divine results, you have to depend on a higher power and realize that worry serves no healthy purpose.

In Matthew 6:25-34, Jesus said, "Therefore I tell you, do not worry about your life, what you will eat or drink or about your body, what you will wear. Is not life more than food and the body more than clothing? Look at the birds of the air; they do not sow or reap, they gather nothing into barns, yet your heavenly Father feeds them. Are you not more important than they? Can any of you by worrying add a single moment to your life? Why are you anxious about clothes? Consider the lilies of the field. They do not toil or spin. But I tell you that not even Solomon, in all his splendor, was clothed like one of them. If God so clothes the grass of the field, which grows today and is thrown into the fire tomorrow, will he not much more provide for you, O you of little faith? So do not worry and say, 'What are we to eat?' or 'What are we to drink?' or 'What are we to wear?' All these things the pagans seek. Your heavenly Father knows your needs. But seek first the kingdom of God and his righteousness and all these things will be given you besides. Do not worry about tomorrow's problems, for today's will be sufficient."

Letting Go of Depression

Worry can be a precursor to depression. A report by the U.S. Surgeon General in 1999 states that among developed nations, including the United States, major depression is the leading cause of disability. Additionally, forecasters predict that 65 percent of employees will suffer some form of depression to the point that it can affect their jobs.

Unfortunately, depression is becoming more common, affecting even teenagers and young children, and the suicide rate is rising. Depression can take away a person's identity and cause them to take their own life. It is a serious illness, but it can be treated successfully. It is one of the few illnesses from which the recovering patient can become stronger and healthier than before.

I believe that depression comes from a feeling of being deprived of something that you want but do not have. This is the same feeling I experienced when I suffered from depression. I wasn't conscious of it, but I felt I deserved more. At that point in my life I should have been making more money. I felt I should have accomplished more. I'd worked hard, and I should have had a better home and a better car. I came to realize that this is what is called "coveting thy neighbor's goods," and it almost destroyed me. Depression leaves an empty heart, and you can't enjoy a full life when your heart is empty.

I want you to understand I'm not saying that if you suffer from depression it is your fault. It doesn't mean that you are a weak person or that you could have prevented it. There can be many underlying causes, but I know from personal experience that a negative thought process can play an important role in developing this illness.

Recognizing Control

One of the biggest restrictions we place on the inflow of God's grace occurs when we try to control everything in our lives. It is good to be in control, but you must recognize the situations in which control is not possible.

You can control your feelings and your emotions, how you react to situations. You can control your destiny, what you choose to do and become. And you can control, in large part, your health. But somewhere, in all of this "being in charge," there is a fine, thin line. Once you cross over this line, you enter a realm where you are no longer in control. In this realm, no matter what you do or how hard you try, you cannot change things. You can't make someone happy who doesn't want to be happy. You cannot change someone who doesn't want to change. You cannot do something for someone else unless they want it done, because this is not your realm: the choices and the ability to change belong to someone else.

Much of our time worrying is spent on things outside of our realm. You worry about your friends, co-workers, boss, family members, children, etc. You worry because you care and you want to help. You must learn that you can only help by listening, assisting them, praying for them and just being there for them. You cannot make someone else happy; happiness comes from within one's own self. You cannot make decisions for someone else. It is impossible for you to do that, no matter how strongly you feel that your choice would be better for them.

The stronger you care about someone, the finer the line becomes and the harder it is to realize when you've crossed over. That is why parents have such a hard time allowing their children to make their own decisions as they grow older. When children are small, they are within your realm. You are the source of their entire existence. You choose what they will wear, what they will eat, who their friends are, where they will go and what they will do each day. But along the way, without your noticing it, they step a little farther away from you until they enter a realm of their own. And the line, for parents, is virtually invisible. This doesn't mean that you stop caring or offering to help them. It simply means learning that this is all you can do. They are the masters of their own realm and the creators of their own destiny.

If we cross over that line and step into someone else's realm and continually try to control these situations, this is where, I feel, we find the source of anxiety, depression, stress, high blood pressure and a host of other ailments. Because when you are in someone else's realm, it is very easy to pick up feelings that don't belong to you. You begin to sympathize with them. If they are angry because they were treated unfairly, you can begin to feel that. If they are sad or depressed, you relate to it and you begin to experience the same feelings and emotions. Before long you're feeling anxious, wondering what you can do, and feeling overwhelmed about a situation that is not even yours to change. You must realize that you have no power in someone else's realm.

We can never control the actions of another person; however, we can control the way we let these actions affect us. There is so much valuable energy that could be used for creative thinking and creative living, but is wasted when tempers get out of control. That merely causes adverse situations to become worse. It's a waste of energy and no one benefits from it.

Think about your own life. Have you crossed over the line? Are you trying to control situations in someone else's realm? Has it caused you to feel anxious, depressed or overwhelmed?

Use your awareness shield; it will clarify the line for you. To help you become even more aware of this line, give it a color. This will make it easier for you to recognize the situations over which you have no control because they are in someone else's realm.

When you feel you've crossed over that line, take a deep breath and say to yourself, "I have no power in this realm. I have no control over this." Cross back over the line, into your own realm, take a deep breath and let it go. Put it in God's hands and let it go completely. Immediately, you will feel the difference.

Every time you put it in God's hands, you're setting yourself free from that bondage and removing the kinks from the hose, thereby allowing the flow of God's healing grace.

Letting Go of Doubt

Doubt is another restriction on what God can do in our lives. When we doubt, we place our human limitations on His divine possibilities. Doubt and our humanness will not let us see beyond the confines of our own tower. But the child, Spirit, can see far beyond the horizon and knows that in God there are no limitations. That is why I've seen the greatest success in working with clients when I help them to release their spirit, breaking free from the chains that bind them, and help their spirit to soar higher than they ever consciously thought possible.

During one of my seminars, a man volunteered for a demonstration on nonverbal suggestions. I asked him if there were any problems he wanted to solve. He told me that he had a problem seeing himself as successful. He was filled with doubts about himself and his capabilities and this prevented him from seeing himself clearly. I proceeded to guide him into an altered state by using only nonverbal suggestions. While in the altered state, I told him that he would feel relaxed and at peace. I then told him, "You are a good person and there is a reason you came here. You may not even be consciously aware of what it is. But here, in this peaceful

165

place, you will find the answer. Now, in the privacy of your own mind, go with holy and empty hands to your God and listen to what He has to say to you." I stepped back and waited for several moments before bringing him out of the hypnotic state. As he opened his eyes, you could see that he had just experienced a profound moment. I asked him if there was anything he'd like to share, and with eyes filled with tears, he said, "I saw Jesus and he told me, 'When you can't see things clearly, see out of my eyes.'" It totally changed his perception.

Letting Go of Critical Judgments

Another way in which we restrict the flow of God's graces is by judging others. We tend to shy away from people who don't live up to our standards or beliefs because they are of a different race or religion, or maybe because we simply don't want to be inconvenienced by them.

I am reminded of a story told by Dr. Art Winkler about a young soldier who was finally coming home after having fought in Vietnam. He called his parents from San Francisco. "Mom and Dad, I'm coming home, but I have a favor to ask. I have a friend I'd like to bring home with me." "Sure," they replied, "we'd love to meet him."

"There's something you should know," the son continued. "He was hurt pretty badly in the fighting. He stepped on a land mine and lost an arm and leg. He has nowhere else to go, and I want him to come live with us." "I'm sorry to hear that, son. Maybe we can help him find somewhere to live." "No, Mom and Dad, I want him to live with us." "Son," said the father, "you don't know what you're asking. Someone with such a handicap would be a terrible burden on us. We have our own lives to live, and we can't let something like this interfere with our lives. I think you should just come home and forget about this guy. He'll find a way to live on his own."

At that point the son hung up the phone. The parents heard nothing more from him. A few days later, however, they received a call from the San Francisco police. Their son had died after falling from a building, they were told. The police believed it was a suicide.

The grief-stricken parents flew to San Francisco and were taken to the city morgue to identify the body of their son. They recognized him, but to their horror, they also discovered something they didn't know. Their son had only one arm and one leg.

If the son had told his parents what had happened to him, they would probably have welcomed him home with open arms. But instead they were quick to judge, and God forbid that they should be burdened with a stranger's problems. Their reaction sent a message to their son that *he* would be a burden.

The next time you are tempted to criticize or judge someone else, remember to "judge not, lest you be judged."

Sometimes we tend to be our own harshest critic. A very dear friend of mine called me up one day. He was experiencing the most difficult trial of his life. He had been married for almost thirty years and his marriage had collapsed. He said his wife had just told him she no longer loved him. And it totally devastated him. He had moved out of the house and asked me to meet him. I went to his motel room and we spoke for a long time. I returned home, and after a few weeks he telephoned me again. He asked me if he could come over and perhaps I could do a session with him. I told him, "Sure. Come on over." As he sat there, he poured his heart out to me. He said that he told his wife to take the house and property. He didn't want any of it. He wanted her to be happy. He kept a few dollars of their savings, and that was basically it. But it began to eat him up inside. What was wrong with him? How did he fail? And the part that really crushed him was that he felt he was losing the love of his children. Although they were grown, they couldn't understand what was happening. They questioned why he had left and he couldn't explain. They didn't believe some of the things that happened and he felt them turning away from him. He had been beating himself up like this for so long, and he just couldn't take any more. I began doing a session with him, and during the session I said, "I'm going to place my hand on your forehead and this is going to help you relax." I do this with each person who comes to me, whether to stop smoking, reduce weight, relieve anxiety, it doesn't matter. There is a time during each session, while the client is in an altered state, that I place my hand on their forehead, and as I do so, I pray quietly. I don't speak out loud, but in my mind I say, "Lord, whatever it is that this person needs to be set free from, let them know it. Touch them in a special way and heal them." And this is where I see miraculous things take place.

As I did this with my friend, he began to shake and I could see tears roll out of the corners of his eyes. I removed my hand from his forehead and continued with the session. When I counted him out of the altered state, I asked if he was okay. He said, "Yeah. Oh man, what an experience!" I asked him if there was anything that he wanted to share. He said, "Definitely! Louie, I was up on a cross and I was hanging there. All of this torment was going through my mind about losing the love of my children, my wife and everything else. I was hanging there, suffering terribly, and I looked down and saw Jesus standing there. He called me by name and said, "Come down off the cross. You've been crucifying yourself long enough."

That was the message that he needed to hear and he was totally changed after that. He forgave all that was done to him, and more importantly, he was able to forgive himself. He was able to release it and let it go, and in doing so, he set his spirit free. I am sorry to say that he is no longer with us, but someone who knew him well said that he lived the rest of his life with unconditional love and became even more spiritual.

When we no longer allow ourselves to be controlled by negative emotions, we raise ourselves above the natural human plane and become more spiritual. By "spiritual," I don't necessarily mean religious. Many atrocities throughout history have taken place in the name of religion. Religion is man-made, but spirituality is God-given. You can debate religions, but spirituality is not debatable because it exists within each of us. It is part of our being. It was created as part of us when our soul first came into existence. Everyone is spiritual, even though they may be at different levels of spirituality. Even non-believers are spiritual. They just have trouble seeing beyond human limitations.

All of the clients who come to me fill out a pre-session form and one of the questions I ask is "What is your religion?" I do this so I know where my clients are coming from and I can help them in the best way possible, without inflicting my own beliefs on them.

An April 2000 Newsweek poll, conducted by Princeton Survey Research Associates, showed that 94 percent of people believe in God and 84 percent believe that God performs miracles.

If 94 percent of people believe in God or a higher power, why not work with that belief for their benefit when conducting therapy?

Miraculous results can take place when a person taps into this higher level of consciousness. I've seen people achieve results on the spiritual level that they were unable to achieve on the physical or emotional level. Once they become in tune with their spirituality, it's as if they open another door or window and receive a breath of fresh air, a new awareness and understanding.

There seems to be a growing awareness in the medical profession of the importance of working with a person's spirituality in the healing process. According to the National Institute for Healthcare Research in Rockville, Maryland, at least forty U.S. medical schools offer a spirituality course aimed at this other dimension of treatment.

One client, who came to me to stop smoking, was a scientist who worked for the Space Center. On his pre-session form, he had written "Atheist." I asked him his opinion on the planets and the universe. Did he feel that there was some kind of force holding everything together? "Most definitely," he said, and he proceeded to go into scientific detail about rotations and magnetic forces. I told him, "Good. Then let's work with that force." I then conducted the session with him, and when he came out of the altered state, he reached into his pocket, took out his pack of cigarettes and threw them into the wastebasket. "I don't need these things anymore," he said. As he was leaving, he turned to me and said,

"Look, I don't know what I just experienced there. I mean, I was really in a wonderful, peaceful place. I've never experienced anything like that before." "Well," I told him, "I guess it would be all right if I say, 'May the force be with you'?" He laughed and said, "Yeah, you could say that." Since then he has referred numerous clients to me.

Just because you don't believe in God, doesn't mean He ceases to exist. During this life's journey, there may be situations that shift our level of spirituality. Remember the old saying during World War II? "There are no atheists in foxholes."

I'm reminded of the story of the atheist who went on a hiking expedition in the Himalayas. It was coming upon evening of the first day and the native scout warned him about the yeti. The atheist laughed and said, "I don't believe in the abominable snowman." He pitched his tent and curled up to rest for the night. Just as he dozed off, he heard a deep snarling growl, and before he could move, his tent was torn in two. A giant hand reached in and picked him up; the next thing he knew, he was dangling in the air, face to face with a twelve-foot yeti. "Oh God, please help me. Save me from this creature." The clouds parted and a voice from heaven said, "I thought you didn't believe in Me." "Yeah, that's true," said the atheist, "but ten minutes ago I didn't believe in him either!"

Some people have trouble accepting anything they can't see, smell, taste or touch. They say, "I have to see it to believe it." Those people will never really experience true joy and peace because, by their doubts, they confine their spirit within human limitations. They don't realize that sometimes "you have to believe it to see it."

171

There's a story about a teacher who was trying to explain evolution to the children in her class. She asked a little boy, "Tommy, do you see the tree outside?" "Yes," answered Tommy. "Good," she said. "Do you see the grass outside?" "Yes," the little boy answered. "Now, go to the window and look up. I want you to tell me if you can see the sky," the teacher told him. Tommy walked over to the window and peered out. "Yes ma'am, I see the sky." "Good. Now, Tommy, when you looked, did you see God?" Tommy shook his head and said, "No." "That's my point, children," said the teacher. "We can't see God because he isn't there. He doesn't exist."

A little six-year-old girl in the back of the room spoke up and said, "Teacher, can I ask Tommy some questions?" The teacher agreed and the little girl asked, "Tommy, do you see the tree outside?" "Yes," Tommy answered. The little girl then asked, "Tommy, do you see the grass?" The little boy, tired of questions by this time, sighed, "Yessss." "Do you see the sky?" she asked him. "Yes," he groaned. "Tommy, do you see the teacher?" "Of course I do," he replied. "Well," she said, "do you see her brain?" "No," said Tommy, shaking his head. The little girl folded her arms and said, "Then, according to what we were taught today, she must not have one!"

"For we walk by faith, not by sight."
(II Corinthians 5:7)

When we become more spiritual, we become more childlike. Just think about the wonderful qualities of a child. Have you ever seen young children fighting? They could be yelling, calling each other names and pushing each other, but five minutes later, they're sitting down with their arms around one another, sharing a cookie. They don't hold grudges, and they don't remember everything the other said the last time they got into a fight, just so that they can throw it up to them later. It's simply forgotten.

Or just watch other children's faces when they see another child crying. They are truly concerned. They may not even know why the other child is crying, but they can feel the child's pain.

Children are trusting and if you tell them something, it has to be so, simply because you said it. Children don't see limits, they see endless possibilities.

And young children are filled with unconditional love. They don't see race or religion. It doesn't matter if you're fat or thin, tall or short. Looks might deter them at first, but not for long because a child has the ability to see what's on the inside.

I understand what Jesus meant when he said, "Unless you become like a little child, you will not enter into the kingdom of heaven." I think he was trying to tell us to release our spirit, the child that is in each of us, and let go of all the negative thoughts and emotions that we tend to hold on to as we grow older. When you release these things, you release your spirit. In doing so, you rise above your humanness and achieve the ability to see things clearly.

A couple of years ago, I took a flight to Washington State. The day we were to leave was plagued with thunderstorms. It was raining and lightning fiercely. I commented to myself that it wasn't a good day for flying. The weather remained terrible, even as we were taking off. As the plane began to climb, the storm raged around us. But before I knew it, we were flying above the storm. The sun was shining brightly and the sky was a vivid blue. As I looked down, I could see the black clouds of the thunderstorm below. I was awed as I looked about me. When I was on the ground, it seemed to be a miserable day, but as the plane flew above the storm, it was actually beautiful. I thought to myself, when you can see the vastness, everything else seems so insignificant.

And it is the same with us. Life seems miserable when you are plagued with negativity. By our attitudes we can create the storms that rage around us. But when we let go of these things, we free our spirit and it soars high above the turmoil and gives us clarity of sight. We can see things as they really are. And I can promise you that once you experience the feeling of freedom that comes through releasing the spirit, you will no longer allow yourself to be held down. You will break free from any chains that bind you, and your spirit will soar high above the green fields, into the limitless blue and far beyond the horizon.

Chapter 11

The Key to Happiness

I want to give you something, something that will release your spirit permanently from bondage. It's a key. This key will unlock any lock and open any door. It's a key to happiness and peace. It's a key to meaning in a world that makes no sense. The key is *forgiveness.*

I can assure you, if you use this key, it will unlock any chains that bind you! And will set you free from all anger, resentment, bitterness, jealousy, depression and revenge. It will give you peace of mind and a healthier body, and will set your spirit free.

Although their beliefs may differ, the world's major religions all share a common thread: their belief in the power of forgiveness.

Forgiveness is not a feeling; it's an act of the will, the free will that God gave us. The good feelings will come later, for they are the by-products of the act of the will.

You can look around you and see that forgiveness is what is needed most in the world today because this world is a world of illusion. The world portrays the illusion that money is power and happiness. It creates the misconception that only youth and the "beautiful people" are acceptable, which makes the majority of us feel inferior. We can't forgive ourselves because we don't live up to others' expectations. The world tells us, "Don't get mad, get even." Living within this illusion strangles the spirit.

Those who forgive release themselves from the illusion and from the world, and those who withhold forgiveness bind themselves to it. By forgiving, you can be *in* the world but not *of* the world. When you forgive, you gain clarity of sight. You break through the illusion and see things as they truly are, and you achieve your own "world peace."

My son-in-law, Bob, and his father never really had a close relationship. His father was the type of man who never showed much affection, and he never told the boy that he loved him. One day his father suffered a heart attack and a stroke. They rushed him to the hospital, but he went into a coma and the doctors said that they didn't expect him to make it through the night. My son-in-law called me, so I went to the hospital to see him.

When I went into the room, my son-in-law was crying. I hugged him and he said, "I don't know what to do." I walked to the other side of the bed and told him, "Do this. Put your hand on his forehead." He did so and I placed my hand over his. "Now, give me your other hand." And we held hands across his dad. I said, "Son, whatever is bound here on earth is going to be bound in heaven. But whatever is turned loose here on earth is going to be loose in heaven. Forgive him. Let it go. And in his own way, he'll be able to be free from it." We prayed together for a while and I left. The next day, his father came out of the coma, and he lived for three more months.

Those three months brought them closer than they had ever been before. Every day, Bob went to the hospital and fed his dad and bathed him. He did everything he could for him. One day, his father reached up and patted his face and said, "I love you, son." What a blessing!

One day Bob was called out of town for his job. There wasn't anything he could do about it. My daughter tried to ease his mind: "It's only for one day. You'll be back this evening and you can come to the hospital when you get home."

He left, and late that afternoon, my daughter called me and said it didn't look like Bob's father was doing too well. I went to the hospital and we prayed. His breathing became more shallow and I said, "He's let it all go. He's free now." We watched him breathe softer and more shallow until he took his last breath.

My son-in-law arrived just moments after his dad had passed. He was understandably upset. But I told him, "He was at peace. He crossed over very peacefully." "But I've been here every day," he said. "And the one day I leave, he passed away." "Don't you see?" I said. "It's almost like he waited until you were gone, as if he chose that time so it wouldn't be so hard on you. He was at peace and he wanted you to be at peace too. You were given a blessing, a period of grace where you both could let go of the mistakes of the past. You did, and it was time to move on."

My son-in-law felt fortunate to have had that "grace period," that chance to forgive. But forgiveness is not simply for the benefit of those who have wronged us. It is actually more beneficial for the one who is forgiving, because through forgiveness you free yourself from whatever is holding you back.

It may not always be easy to forgive. I know that because I myself experienced that inner battle. I didn't deserve all that had happened to me. Why should I forgive them and let them off the hook? But remember, the choice for happiness is yours to make. You must be willing to let it go. By forgiving those who had hurt me, what I had really done was to let myself off the hook.

In Matthew 26:39, Jesus said, "Father, if it is possible, let this cup pass from me." There was an inner battle going on within him. A little later he prayed again, saying, "Father, if it is not possible that this cup pass without me drinking it, Your will be done." He turned it all over to God the Father. He ended the battle.

Take a moment now and think; is there a battle going on in your life? Is there someone who has wronged you in some way and you're still allowing it to control your way of life? If so, maybe it's time to let it go and let yourself off the hook.

I realize now that, in the chapel that night, I was willing to forgive—to forgive all those who had hurt me and to forgive myself. I didn't like the person I had become, and I didn't want to feel that way anymore. So in my own crude way, I was forgiving. Through forgiveness, I was open to Jesus and his healing grace, and it was then that he touched me and set me free. He gave me peace of mind, he healed my body (putting the chemicals back in balance), but most of all he set my spirit free.

Matthew 22:35-40 tells us, "And one of them (a scholar of the law) asked Jesus a question, to test him. 'Teacher, which is the greatest commandment in the law?' And Jesus said to him, 'You shall love the Lord your God with all your heart, and with all your soul, and with all your mind. This is the greatest and first commandment. The second is like it, you shall love your neighbor as yourself. On these two commandments depend all the law and the prophets.'"

I can imagine the scholar saying, "*NO*, I only want to know what is the first and most important commandment." But Jesus, almost in the same breath, said, "The second most important commandment is to love your neighbor as yourself." That seems to fly right over our heads. Did we not understand what Jesus meant? Sometimes, if we loved our neighbor as we love ourselves, our neighbors would be in terrible shape. Jesus was saying, love yourself. You were created in the image and likeness of God. You are a child of God. Jesus said the kingdom of God is within you.

Sometimes it's easier for us to forgive others than to forgive ourselves. We hold on to guilt or anger and literally become our own worst enemy.

I worked with a client, Arthur, a Vietnam vet who was plagued with feelings of rage, betrayal and guilt. He was consumed with feelings of rage against the government for not letting them do their job in Vietnam. He felt betrayed by the country he fought for and so many died for because of the treatment they received when they returned home. And for years he carried around feelings of guilt because he returned when so many others didn't. He didn't realize it, but thirty years later, he was still fighting the war, only now he had become the enemy.

During the war, he was a Naval airplane captain. Not only did he fly the planes but it was also his job to check them over before they went out. "When a plane didn't come back," he said, "I felt that maybe it was my fault because I didn't do something right. Maybe I didn't check it close enough. And I would go outside and cry like a baby. The

179

men who died had mothers, fathers, sisters, brothers, wives and babies back home, and I always felt guilty because I came home when they didn't. There isn't a day goes by that I don't think about my guys that didn't make it home. It's so bad I find myself checking everything at the house—the doorknobs, the stove, everything over and over again so that nothing happens to my family."

During the session, I worked with him on forgiveness. His quality of life had suffered because not only couldn't he forgive the government, he couldn't forgive himself.

After the session, it was like looking at a different man. His whole attitude and demeanor had changed. He said, "Doc, it's like a huge weight's been lifted off me! While I was under, I saw myself standing in front of the hangar where we used to keep the planes. It was this huge dome building and I was afraid to go in. I knew that all the guys I let down, the ones who didn't make it home, were going to be in there. But I felt compelled to go in. When I walked in, the hangar was empty. No one was there. But I heard them say, 'Why have you been worried about us? We're in a better place. You've carried our load around long enough. Get on with your life and be happy. You never let any of us down. We love you, man. Thanks for caring all these years.' Boy, that was quite an experience! It was wonderful!"

I told him that this was just the beginning and he would notice other good things happening to him.

The next day I received a telephone call from him. He said, "I just had to call and tell you what happened to me last night. When I got home, I was thinking about my old flight suit. I didn't know where it was because it wasn't something I wanted to look at before. It brought back too many bad memories. But I decided to go look for it. I went up in the attic and as I was looking for the light, I stumbled on something. When I turned on the light, I was shocked to see that what I stumbled on was my old flight suit, just lying there on the floor! I picked it up and put it on, and I can't tell you the feeling I had. I was engulfed in happiness and I had a feeling of freedom that I hadn't felt in years! I just started crying out of pure happiness. It's like I found myself for the first time in a very long time. I had my wife take a picture of me in it, and you know, the strange part is that it still fits!"

A month later, I received a Christmas card from him and enclosed was the picture of him in his flight suit. He's standing there, beaming, with his arms raised high in the air. It is a picture I cherish because I know firsthand the joyous feeling of release that comes through forgiveness.

The card also touched me deeply because it was another affirmation of the power of forgiveness. There, printed in small letters at the bottom of the card, was the scripture quote "… I am come that they might have life, and they might have it more abundantly."

Through his actions during his crucifixion, Jesus teaches the importance of forgiveness. And I have seen firsthand the awesome power that forgiveness has, not only to change lives but also to give life and give it abundantly.

Why hold on to all that anger? Why not do what Jesus did, as he hung on the cross? He said, *"Forgive them, Father, for they know not what they do."* Can you imagine all of the physical and emotional pain he was experiencing at that time? And yet, even with all the pain, he was willing to forgive. That proves that forgiveness is not a feeling, it is an act of the will. Who are we to hold on to anger and unforgiveness, when Jesus himself was willing to forgive? Jesus did not deserve all the things that were happening to him, yet he was willing to forgive. The resurrection came through forgiveness. And the same is true with you. Through forgiveness you can be resurrected to a new life, a new meaning, a new purpose.

Several years ago, Jim, a client experiencing strong emotional problems, came to me. His intense feelings of anger were eating him up, causing him to feel depressed. We began sessions for release and forgiveness, but even after several sessions, he was still unable to let go of those negative emotions.

One evening, after the fifth session, his wife called to inform me that he had had a heart attack. They had taken him to the hospital and he was asking for me. It was impossible for me to go up there that evening or the next day, because of other clients, but I assured her that I would be there as soon as I could. The following evening, I went to the hospital to see him. When I arrived, he was sitting up in bed and his wife was sitting in the corner chair, reading a newspaper.

I smiled at him, pulled up a chair by his bed and we began talking. It wasn't long before we began discussing the importance of forgiveness again. "Look," I told him, "it isn't important. All of the feelings you're holding on to just aren't important. The only thing that matters is that you're at peace—at peace with yourself, at peace with God and at peace with others." We talked for over an hour. As I was getting ready to leave, I walked over to get my coat, and as I turned around I saw him getting out of the bed. "Wait, is it all right for you to get out of bed?" I asked. "Oh, the doctor said it's okay if he gets up, to go to the bathroom," his wife replied. As I looked at him, I felt compelled to give him a hug, so I walked over to him, hugged him and said, "I love you, Jim."

As I said this, I felt his body go limp in my arms. He slumped down toward the floor and his wife screamed. The nurses came in and called a code on him. His wife and I went out into the hall and waited.

About forty-five minutes later, the doctor came out and said, "Are you Louis?" "Yes," I answered. "Well, he's asking for you. He had an out-of-body experience. When we went in, he was flatline. We couldn't get the heart to beat. We shocked him three times, and when we got him back, the first thing he said was, 'Why did you bring me back?'"

I went into the room. Jim was weak and could hardly move, but he tried to reach out his hand. I walked over to him, held his hand and put my head on the pillow next to his. "God's not finished with you yet. He's got some plans for you," I told him.

Jim pulled through, and his wife said that he was completely changed after that experience. He was no longer angry and it was a pleasure just to be around him.

I would see him from time to time, and one day he told me that although he was retired he still kept busy by going to get groceries for people who couldn't get out. He just had a desire to help people. Not long after that, both he and his wife became ordained ministers. He's still around and going strong. I guess you could say I've seen the dead rise through the power of forgiveness.

Forgiveness is not a one-time act. In Matthew 18:21-22, Peter came up and said to Jesus, "Lord, how often shall my brother sin against me, and I forgive him? As many as seven times?" Jesus said to him, "I do not say to you seven times, but seventy times seven."

Peter wanted a number. It's as if Peter needed to know that there was a limit to the amount of abuse he had to accept.

Just like the rest of us, he could probably forgive someone once, maybe even twice, but here was Jesus suggesting that more was required. "Do you mean if he continues to hurt me, I have to bend so far as to forgive him seven times?" "No, Peter, not seven times, but *seventy* times seven." This probably blew Peter's mind! I can almost imagine him saying, "Wait, that's not fair!" Jesus was trying to tell Peter that we don't need to keep a tally of how many times we forgive. We must forgive so often that it would be impossible to keep track of.

Forgiveness is ongoing and necessary when someone says something to you that hurts, when someone does something to you that wasn't right and you didn't deserve it, when you are driving behind a little old lady doing twenty miles an hour in a forty-mile zone, when somebody pulls out in front of you and has the audacity to give you the finger, or when you do everything to help someone and they abuse you. Think about it. What forgiveness is needed in your life? The choice is yours. Be willing to forgive. It's controlled your way of life long enough.

I remember glancing at a magazine one day. I can't recall the name of it or anything between the covers, but I do remember the front. On it was a picture of three veterans in camouflage, hugging one another in front of the Vietnam Wall, and the caption read, "One ex-prisoner of war asked another, 'Have you forgiven your captors yet?' And the other one answered, 'No, never!' 'Then it seems like they still have you in prison, don't they?' he replied."

Life is too precious and too short to be wasted as a prisoner of unforgiveness. Make the decision today to be reconciled with the people in your life who have hurt you or failed you, and be reconciled with yourself. When you do, you not only release them, but you also set your spirit free.

I remember reading somewhere that the holiest place on earth is where an ancient hatred has become a *present love*. When you forgive, you are truly on holy ground.

Some people will say, "I can forgive, but I can't forget." True forgiveness requires letting go completely. Holding on to the memory of the hurt, pain, anger or feelings of betrayal you experienced leaves you in a vulnerable position. Because these feelings and emotions were never truly released, they are always close to the surface. Anything can trigger these negative emotions and cause you to re-experience them, sometimes with a stronger intensity.

Have you ever felt that you were completely over a situation that had caused you pain? And then, out of the blue, you see a picture of the person who was the source of that pain, or just hear their name. Suddenly, it feels as if time had reversed, and you're feeling those negative emotions gnawing away at you all over again. If left unchecked, these feelings will run rampant and eventually consume you. That's what comes from "forgiving and not forgetting."

I'm sure most people are familiar with the Lord's Prayer. I wonder how many of them really pay attention to what they're asking as they pray these words.

Our Father, who art in heaven,
Hallowed be thy name.
Thy kingdom come, thy will be done
On earth, as it is in heaven.
Give us this day our daily bread,
and forgive us our trespasses

185

(Now here comes the sticky part!)
AS WE FORGIVE THOSE WHO TRESPASS AGAINST US.

Do you really want to be forgiven by God in the same way that *you* forgive others? It's a very sobering thought. Take a look at your own life. When you forgive, do you truly let it go? Or do you have a tendency to hold on to it because you "didn't deserve it" or "it wasn't fair"?

One of the cutest stories I've heard concerned a six-year-old girl who was overheard reciting the Lord's Prayer at a church service. She recited it beautifully until she got to the part "… and forgive us our *trash passes*, as we forgive those who *passed trash* against us." Although she didn't quote it accurately, she certainly had the gist of it correct. She seemed to understand the point that Jesus was trying to get across better than most grown-ups do—out of the mouth of babes!

In Luke 6:36-38, Jesus said, "Be compassionate, as your father is compassionate. Do not judge and you will not be judged. Do not condemn and you will not be condemned. Pardon and you shall be pardoned. Give and it shall be given unto you. Good measure pressed down, shaken together, running over will they pour into the fold of your garment. *For the measure you measure with, will be measured back to you.*" Is this a confirmation that "what goes around, comes around"?

I remember hearing a story about how God forgives us. Imagine when you die, Jesus comes to meet you and shows you a video of your entire life. On the video you see all the good things you did. But there are also a number of blanks on the tape. You ask why there are so many blanks on the tape of your life and Jesus tells you that these were the times when you sinned and asked for God's mercy. When God forgives, He completely blanks out our sins and does not remember.

Unfortunately, we have difficulty doing the same. We tend to just push it off to the side and think that we've forgiven, when actually we allow the hurt or anger we felt about the situation to control us. Until we let go completely, these negative feelings can still have an adverse effect on our lives.

Imagine sweeping your house clean, but instead of getting rid of the dirt, you just sweep it under a rug. Every day you sweep the house and every day you push a little more dirt under the rug; eventually the dirt mounds so high underneath that it causes a bump on the rug and whenever you walk past that spot, you have a tendency to stumble. If the dirt is not removed completely, it will eventually cause you to fall.

In much the same way, unless you completely let go of past hurts, they can cause future problems.

You must understand that even though you forgive, you may sometimes re-experience those negative thoughts or emotions. That's just part of human nature. The difference is that forgiveness brings a new awareness that helps you to see them for what they are, merely thoughts or emotions. You might still feel them from time to time, but they no longer have the power to take root because your heart is filled with something even more powerful: forgiveness.

In Matthew 12:43-45, Jesus said, "When an unclean spirit departs from a person, it roams through arid regions searching for rest, but it can not find any. So it says to itself, 'I'll go back to the place from which I came,' and upon returning it finds everything empty, swept clean and all in order. Then it goes off and brings back with itself several other spirits, even more evil than itself, and they dwell there and the last condition of that person is worse than the first."

Previously, when I read this scripture, it was frightening to think that a person could actually become filled with even more evil spirits and be worse off than before. Then one day when I read it again, it was as if a veil had been lifted and I could truly understand this prophetic warning.

Unresolved anger, bitterness, resentment, jealousy, revenge and guilt are all unclean spirits—demons. When you use your free will and make a conscious decision to forgive, you release yourself from those demons. What you need to also understand is that these demons occupy a space within a person, and when they depart, they leave a void. Unless that void is filled with something else, something good—such as God, love, compassion and forgiveness—painful memories and negative thoughts and feelings can take root again, but this time they'll take over completely. Then, not only will the previous negative feelings return, but other, worse ones will be created, such as hatred and even depression. You can see how the second condition would be worse than the first.

Recently, I received another letter from Arthur, the Vietnam vet I told you about earlier. In this correspondence, his wife explained that he was experiencing some physical problems and struggling with some emotional ones. He wanted to go to sleep, because in his words, "While I sleep it's like I'm fighting a battle with the evil one and I have to finish this battle."

Maybe it was the strain of a physical problem, or perhaps he felt those old feelings of rage and guilt trying to come back and consume him, but whatever it was, it literally gave him the feeling that he had to fight a battle.

As I was about to leave on a trip, I vowed to call him upon my return. The trip took me to Tallahassee, Florida, where I was scheduled to speak to a church group about the power of forgiveness. During the talk, I shared with them the story of Arthur and how his life was changed through forgiveness.

Afterward, a man came up to me, crying. "You know," he said, "I was also in Vietnam and I was experiencing many of the same things as that other man you told us about. But suddenly, it's gone. I feel free of it now."

Upon my return, I called Arthur and he told me that he was feeling better.

"Well, congratulations, Arthur," I told him. "I'm happy for you! There's something else I want to share with you. For so many years, you felt guilty for not bringing more boys home. Well, you can completely let go of that now because through your story, another Vietnam vet was released from those same feelings. You won the battle. You just brought another one home."

He was deeply moved and pleased to realize that he could help someone else through his experience. And he had overcome his battle. He didn't allow those negative feelings to take over again.

I can understand how those thoughts and feelings have a tendency to come back, because I myself experienced them. But I recognize them now and I no longer give them any power.

Once you forgive, if you experience negative thoughts and feelings trying to return, recognize them for what they are and stand firm. Do not give them any power to affect your life. Say to yourself, or even voice it out loud, "Get out of here! There is no room for you anymore!" Once you do this, you take control of the situation instead of allowing it to control you.

By holding on to negative emotions, by not forgiving and releasing them, we can actually create a physical illness that is harmful to us. In my case, because I had allowed anger and resentment to constantly replay in my mind, I created a chemical imbalance that, in turn, caused the depression. Forgiveness freed me from that bondage and brought harmony back to my mind, body and spirit.

Did you ever hear a doctor tell you to forgive your neighbor in order to cure your tension headaches or lower your blood pressure? Probably not, because many people, even professionals, do not realize the positive effect that forgiveness has on the body. Hopefully, some day soon, they will.

If you have a sickness called anger, then have your doctor prescribe a medication called gratitude. You can't be angry and thankful at the same time.

I would venture to say that anger is the only emotion people are unlikely to want to change.

You may ask yourself, "Why should I forgive?" Then you should also ask yourself another question, "Why not?" What do you have to gain by holding on to hatred? You, the hater, could die of a heart attack or stroke, while those you hate live a long healthy life because they are unburdened by those negative emotions.

Now I want you to ask yourself another question, "If I allow bitterness and resentment to take over my thoughts, whom does it affect?" Consistently dwelling on these negative feelings can weaken your immune system, causing you to develop a serious illness or depression, while the person you felt was unfair to you remains healthy. *Your* quality of life suffers, not theirs. When you look at it like this, it's clear to see whose life is affected.

If you can forgive and let go of the anger and resentment, peace will take its place and your life will become more fulfilled and rewarding.

When many of my clients finally release themselves from their unresolved anger, they begin crying pitifully, like a little child, much the same as I did that night in the chapel when I forgave those who had hurt me.

Many of them immediately want to apologize for their tears, but I tell them it's okay to cry. Even Jesus wept. Are we supposed to be stronger than him?

Crying is cleansing and can actually be good for us. Did you know that crying can actually remove chemicals that build up in the body during emotional stress? According to biochemist William Frey, our moods can be affected by the amount of manganese that is stored in our body. Thirty times more manganese is found in tears than in blood serum. The lachrymal gland determines the flow of tears and concentrates and removes manganese from the body. And there are three other chemicals, besides manganese, that are built up by the body during stress and released by crying.

So you see, crying doesn't make you weak; it can actually make you healthy.

In Luke 10, Jesus said to his disciples, "I send you out like lambs among wolves." That's a serious prospect. He knew how difficult it was going to be and how hard it would be to remain a lamb when surrounded by wolves. He also told his disciples, "Into whatever house you enter, first say, 'Peace to this house.' If a peaceful person lives there, your peace will rest on him, but if not, take your peace back." In other words, if you offer your peace to someone and they try to give you back something else, such as anger or hatred, don't take it. Don't become angry or bitter in return, and don't let their reactions become yours. Simply hold on to your peace and remain a lamb among wolves.

In the same chapter, Jesus later told them, "Whatever town you enter and they do not receive you, go and shake their dust from your sandals." Basically he was telling them, "Go into a town, do what you have to do and if they don't receive you, leave and shake it off. Don't carry around with you any negative thoughts or emotions, like 'That wasn't fair' or 'I didn't deserve to be treated like that.' Simply take back your peace, shake it all off and continue on your way."

Many times, throughout life, we find it difficult to just shake it off. We begin to carry around a tremendous amount of unnecessary baggage, such as hard feelings, resentment, anger, guilt, fear and feelings of inadequacy. And we wonder why we feel so burdened and weighted down! Remember, forgiveness is the key to releasing yourself from that bondage.

I want to share with you a meditation technique that many of my clients have found helpful for getting rid of their negative excess baggage. As you read this, go along with it and imagine yourself in the scene.

"No Digging Here" Technique

I want you to use your imagination, and think of yourself walking down a beautiful country road. The sun is shining and the sky is a vivid shade of blue. Soft white clouds drift gently across the sky. It's a wonderful day, and as you walk, you notice the wildflowers along each side of the road. Some of the wildflowers are red and their sweet fragrance fills the air. Whenever you see red flowers, it will remind you of this place.

It's such a beautiful place, and in front of you is an open field. In this field there is one large tree, its giant limbs waving gently in the breeze. You walk toward the shade of the tree, and as you draw close, you notice there is a shovel leaning against the trunk. What color is your shovel?

In the comfort of the shade of the tree, you begin to dig a hole with the shovel. You can dig it as deep as you wish.

Now I want you to take all those things that have been bothering you, all the stress and anger that you've been holding on to; release them and drop them in the hole.

Now take any resentment that you feel toward anyone; release it and drop it in the hole.

If you've been carrying around any guilt or doubt, release it also and drop it in the hole.

If you've been feeling useless or inadequate, let go of those feelings and drop them in the hole.

You don't need to carry those around anymore.

Now, think for a moment. Is there anything else that is bothering you or stopping you from being the person you want to be? If so, drop it in the hole.

Now take your shovel and bury all those things in the hole.

All the things holding you back are now gone. When you put them in the hole, you put them in God's hands. And when you release them into His hands, He buries them forever. He forgives you and sets you free from them.

As you look around under the tree, you notice a sign that says, "NO DIGGING HERE." Notice the color of the letters.

Now take the sign and stick it in the ground over the hole.

If any of those stressful or negative thoughts try to come back into your mind, you will say to yourself, "NO DIGGING HERE." They are in God's hands. That sets you free, and gives you peace of mind.

You feel so much better now that you've released them and let them go. They controlled your way of life long enough and you will allow "NO DIGGING HERE." You are free.

This meditation technique is an invaluable tool to help you release those things that have held you back and prevented you from being the person that God created you to be. Forgiveness is truly the key to unlocking any chains that bind you.

"... forgive us our trespasses
as we forgive those who trespass against us."

Chapter 12

The Value of Meditation

"The Ultimate PTA Meeting"

In today's fast-paced society, our lives are becoming more hectic. Many times it seems as if life's journey is nothing more than a race against the clock. It's not that time is passing any faster. There are still twenty-four hours in a day, seven days in a week and so on. But life seems to be racing past us faster than the speed of light, simply because we keep trying to squeeze more and more into each day.

From the time we open our eyes in the morning until the time we drift off to sleep at night, we run from project to project. Wake up, get dressed, get the kids off to school, go to work, clean the house, run errands, pay bills, go to board meetings, PTA meetings, soccer games, baseball games, football games, music lessons, dance lessons, mow the lawn, plant the garden, change the oil, wash the car, cook the meal, do homework, laundry—whew! And finally, when you lay your head on your pillow at night, before you go to sleep, chances are you're reviewing tomorrow's plans.

We're like the little dog in the story in Chapter 1. We spend so much time being sidetracked that it's very easy to lose focus. We not only lose sight of our destination, the goal we want to achieve, but we also lose sight of ourselves, who we truly are. We seldom take time for ourselves, and if we do, we feel guilty that we should have been doing something else.

There are certain things we do each day that come as naturally to us as breathing and sleeping. These routines, such as bathing, brushing our teeth, flossing, combing our hair and shaving, we take for granted because we've done them all of our lives. Why? It's because we were taught to do so. These routines may not be necessary for survival, but we continue doing them because they make us feel better and they improve our overall well-being.

There is one more thing that we need to incorporate into our daily routine that is just as important as any of these others to our personal growth and well-being. And that is personal time. By "personal time" I mean taking quiet time for yourself, either by using meditation, prayer, imagery, visualization or self-hypnosis.

Personal time, in the context in which I'm speaking, does not include outside distractions such as watching television, talking on the phone, etc. These things, though enjoyable to you, are not beneficial to your personal growth and well-being. It is only through personal time, without any outside distractions, that we can get in touch with the part of ourselves we unknowingly suppress, our true nature. It is during this quiet time that we find truth, answers to our questions and solutions to our problems, and experience true peace and love.

196

Have you ever driven your car for a long time and experienced no problems with it whatsoever? Then one day you get into your car, put the key into the ignition, turn it on but nothing happens. When you get the car to your mechanic, he tells you there is something wrong with your charging system. He hooks your battery up to a charger and suddenly the car starts up and runs great. The battery just needed to be recharged.

We are much the same way. We can go on and on, doing things for others, feeling proud of ourselves that we're so capable, but sooner or later we can run down. We begin to feel dissatisfied, like something is missing, or we may feel tired and irritable. Taking some personal time is like recharging our batteries. It rejuvenates the body, calms the mind and refreshes the spirit.

Meditation, imagery, prayer, visualization and self-hypnosis are all techniques that help us to recharge. The common thread they all share is that they help us to quiet the "chatter" that fills our minds.

"Mind chatter" is the everyday thoughts that consume us: What do I have to get done today? next week? What's happening in my relationships? my friends' relationships? Who said what? What am I going to wear? The list is endless and it occurs constantly, without us even being aware of it. The problem with mind chatter is that it absorbs our focus and attention and prevents us from seeing beyond the here and now. We begin to view things from only one perspective and we lose sight of the fact that there is something greater, a higher existence. Through meditation we calm the chatter and are able to see things clearly, from a more knowledgeable, spiritual point of view.

Think of it this way. Every day, we are surrounded by radio waves. These waves bounce around the atmosphere, carrying music and information that we cannot hear, until we tune in to them with a receptor that can pick up their wave frequencies, such as a radio. When you first turn the radio on, you may hear nothing but static. As you continue turning the knob, you begin hearing a few garbled words and fuzzy music, and suddenly you achieve clarity. The beautiful music resonates in your ears and you are able to distinguish every sharp, crisp note. Everything is clear and you are able to hear things that you couldn't hear before.

We are the same way. God is always with us. He surrounds us. He has the answers to our questions and the solutions to our problems, but most of the time we are unable to hear Him. It is only when we fine-tune our receptor, our mind, that we remove the static and achieve clarity. The blessings are always there, but it is only in that quiet time that we are open to receive them. When we tune in, we leave the things of the outside world and go within and tap into that spiritual part of our being.

When our mind is quiet we are open to receive God's healing grace. That healing grace is always there, but it cannot come into a mind that is at war with itself. Through meditation we learn to release ourselves from those negative thoughts and emotions that rage within us and prevent us from experiencing true peace.

Psalms 46:10 says, "Be still and know that I am God." Unfortunately, we've lost the simple ability to just be still. Our minds are consumed with thoughts of things we have to do, schedules we have to keep. We feel frustrated because there doesn't seem to be enough time to do it all. We are overwhelmed because we keep trying to control everything in our lives and everyone else's and are unable to do so. "Be still and know that I am God." It was only after my own healing that I realized the awesome importance of that statement and began taking that personal time and meditating. Through meditation, I learned something else. I learned that He is God and I am not. I can't handle everything. I can't do it all on my own. But when I allow myself to be quiet and open, He will give me the answers that I need.

After my healing, I went back to school and began studying hypnotherapy. It was tough going in the beginning. I was using our savings to live on while going to school. After I finished school I continued with my internship because this is what I really felt God wanted me to do. When I completed my internship, I went to doctors' offices and asked if they could refer people to me. I explained to them how I could help their patients quit smoking and also relieve stress and anxiety. Most of them politely took my card and information, but that's as far as it went. One told me that he couldn't refer people to me for liability reasons.

Things got even worse. Some of my friends made fun of my new profession. And I even had some people in my own church turn away from me because they said I shouldn't do hypnosis, as it isn't "of God." I became plagued with doubts. I was worried about an income. How would I get clients? Nobody was coming. After all my efforts, did I make a mistake?

I can remember it all so clearly. I went into my office and sat in the recliner. I leaned back, closed my eyes, took a few deep breaths and said, "Heavenly Father, hold me because I really need to be held right now. I thought that this is what you wanted me to do. I felt that this is how you wanted me to help people, but maybe it was my thoughts and not yours. So whatever it is that you want me to do, you're going to have to tell me. And no matter what it is, I'll do it because I truly want to help others. So tell me what it is that you want me to do."

I can't tell you how long I sat in that chair. Other thoughts tried to come into my mind, like "I need to cut the grass" or "There are pine needles on the roof," etc. But I didn't dwell on them. I just sat there quietly and let them flow in and out of my mind.

Suddenly a thought, so powerful that I knew it wasn't mine, came to me: *"There are three things that I want you to do. First, I want you to help everyone who comes to you to realize that the kingdom of God is within them. The second is that when they become aware of this, they will go out and share it with others in their own way, not yours; leave it in My hands. And the third thing I want you to do is to let everyone realize and recognize the power of a thought."* And suddenly, I was filled with peace and I knew that He would take care of me. In that quiet moment, He had given me the answer that I needed.

At the time, I still didn't quite understand what it all meant. I didn't know exactly what I had to do or how to do it. But I knew it was in His hands. Soon everything just started falling into place. The people began coming, and today there are over fifty doctors who refer people to me, as well as many priests and pastors. I work with people in hospitals and wellness centers, dealing with fibromyalgia, cancer, panic and anxiety, grief, depression and pain management. I've done countless seminars and teaching sessions, focusing on the body–mind–spirit connection. And He has taken care of me each step of the way. And since that time, no matter what a person comes to me for, whether it is to stop smoking or to

200

overcome anxiety or depression, I help them to realize that the kingdom of God is within them. Even though they may not consciously believe that they can accomplish that goal or make that change, I help them to realize that there is a power within them, stronger than themselves, which will help them to accomplish anything.

Through that encounter I realized the importance of meditation, of taking that quiet time to tune out the world and tune in to the spirit. "Be still and know that I am God." What a beautiful and awesome statement!

When I work with people using hypnosis, it is nothing more than a guided meditation. I help them to get rid of all the mind chatter and simply guide them into an altered state of consciousness where they are open to receive the answers. You don't need a hypnotherapist to do it. It is something you can do yourself, on a daily basis. I recommend taking at least twenty minutes a day for personal quiet time. Many people bristle at this idea and I constantly hear the same response: "I just can't find the time to do that."

Here's the thing I want you to remember: You don't "find" time, you "make" time. You don't hear people say, "You have to excuse my bad breath, I couldn't find time to brush my teeth" or "I'm sorry I smell, but I couldn't find the time to bathe." No, people *make* the time to do these things because it is important to their personal health and general well-being. The same should be true for meditation. Once you begin to make this part of your daily routine, you will feel so much better that not only will you look forward to it, you will probably increase the time you spend doing it! It is so peaceful and relaxing that most clients, when I bring them out of a session, say, "Gee, I wish I could have stayed there longer."

Another problem that many people have with taking time for meditation is that they feel guilty about taking any time for themselves. One person told me, "Oh, I have so much to do, I would feel selfish taking that much time for myself." It is all well and good to do things for others, but it is also imperative that you make time for yourself. You don't feel guilty when you do things for your children. Why then should you feel guilty about doing something for you, their caregiver?

If you still feel guilty about taking the time to meditate, or if you feel funny telling someone else about it, say instead, "I'm going to my '**PTA**' meeting." It is your **P**ersonal **T**ime **A**wareness meeting, and it is extremely important because it is through this time that you will gain a new awareness and perception. You will find that things no longer affect you the same way. You are calmer and more able to let go of the things that are truly unimportant. And the benefits you receive will have a profound effect not only on you but also on those around you. It will improve your dealings with other people and, more importantly, your relationship with God. Proverbs 14:30 says it best: "A tranquil mind gives life to the body, but jealousy rots the bones."

Do it for you. Think about it. Maybe it's about time you did something for yourself. Remember when Jesus said, "Love your neighbor as yourself"? You must be kind to yourself first and then you can be kind to others.

Jesus himself knew the importance of praying, meditating and simply communicating with his Father. Although he spent his time in the service of others, preaching to them, teaching them or healing them, he still took that time to go off alone and pray. He removed himself from earthly distractions so he could become one with his Father. Sometimes he went off alone, to the desert or even to the garden. And this personal time strengthened him.

When you meditate, go to a quiet place. It can be a special room or perhaps a garden, anywhere you won't be disturbed by outside distractions. You may want to designate a certain room where you meditate regularly. You can create your own space, your own atmosphere. You may want to incorporate certain pictures, plants, candles or soothing music. Whatever makes you feel good.

Matthew 6:6 says, "But when you pray, go to your inner room, close the door and pray to your Father in secret. And your Father who sees in secret will repay you." It really doesn't matter where you meditate. The only important thing is that you go within. Remember, "The kingdom of God is within you."

Meditation is a simple technique, but as with everything else, we have a tendency to make things harder than they are. Keep it simple. There's no big formality to it and you don't have to try to make anything happen.

There are many ways to enter a meditative state. Some people may be able to enter a relaxing state by just removing themselves from any source of distraction. They can enter that peaceful, contemplative state almost immediately. For most, that requires some practice. Some people find it helpful to use a mantra. A mantra is a word or series of words that, when repeated, help eliminate mind chatter by taking the focus away from everyday thoughts. These words can be spoken or sung out loud or simply thought to yourself. It is best to find a quiet place where you can sit and relax. It is also helpful to close your eyes because it eliminates distractions. Begin by noticing your breathing. You don't have to concentrate on it, simply be aware of it. Then begin using your mantra. Some people will use the word "Om," but there is no particular mantra that is better than others. Use whatever you find comfortable, whatever helps you. Looking back on it, I realize that during my first meditation, my mantra was "Heavenly Father, hold me." Another phrase I sometimes use is "Thank you, Jesus." I find that particularly calming and soothing, but someone else may not.

Remember, you don't have to concentrate on the mantra. It is simply used to help you reduce the constant mind chatter. Once you achieve that open, relaxed state, it is no longer necessary to use the mantra; it is up to you. If you should find your mind drifting back to the everyday thoughts, simply begin using your mantra again to help bring you back to that peaceful state.

Another way in which I meditate is to just sit back, close my eyes and think of all my blessings. It is very easy to lose sight of how good life is while we are in the midst of turmoil. This form of meditation reaffirms the goodness of life and reminds us that things are not always as bad as they seem.

The most important thing to remember is to keep your meditations positive. If you constantly ponder how bad things are going in your life, don't expect to see an improvement. Your life will be exactly how you perceive it, and your blessings will remain hidden behind a wall of false perceptions. In the Bible, Philippians 4:8 states, "Finally, brethren, whatever is true, whatever is honest, whatever is just, whatever is pure, whatever is lovely, whatever is gracious, if there is any virtue and if there is anything worthy of praise, meditate on these things."

Imagery can be a powerful tool for helping us to improve our health and achieve our goals. Einstein once said,

"Our imagination is more powerful than knowledge." But imagery and visualization is like a double-edged sword. It can make you ill or it can make you well. Remember, negative thoughts are a form of meditation that can be destructive. People use imagery every day; unfortunately, it is most commonly used in its destructive form, worrying. People will visualize all the bad things that *could* happen, and without their realizing it, it has an adverse effect on the quality of their life.

Imagery is different from normal daydreaming. When people daydream, they are content with their dreams and therefore not motivated to achieve them. It is no more than wishful thinking. But when people use imagery, they imagine their goal and expect to achieve it. This expectation is a form of faith that motivates them into action to make that dream become a reality. Remember the old saying, "If you begin to knit, God will furnish the yarn."

Whenever I am searching for an answer or for guidance, I use meditation. As I sit there with my eyes closed, I ask, "What should I do?" Sometimes as I do this, everyday thoughts try to creep in, but I just let them flow in and out. Eventually I receive the answer. Sometimes the answer doesn't come to me as I'm meditating. It may come later on that night or even the next day. It may even come in a dream as I'm sleeping. I am not consciously trying to receive the answer at the time, it just comes to me. I've learned to keep a tape recorder by my bed so that when I receive information, I can easily record it. The next morning, or days later, I am usually surprised by the valuable information I recorded but consciously forgot.

Each time I meditate, my spirit feels as if it is going home because in that quiet place I find my true self and I become more in tune with my Creator. The more I meditate, the more open I become, and the more open I become, the more graces I receive. It's a continuous renewing cycle.

Meditation is to the soul as rain is to the parched earth. It refreshes, renews and restores, and gives life, so make the time to experience its benefits each day.

I believe that in that quiet, peaceful state, God speaks to us. Some people have trouble accepting this. "Oh, it's all right to talk to God," they say, that's prayer, "but if He talks to you, that's *weird*!" I'm not talking about hearing an audible voice booming from the heavens, but more like a powerful thought, a "knowing" or an insight.

Just remember to be still and be open. There is a story about Elijah in the Old Testament. He took shelter in a cave and was told to go out and stand on the mountain before the Lord as He passed by. Elijah heard a strong and heavy wind rending the mountains and crushing the rocks, but the Lord was not in the wind. After the wind there was an earthquake, but the Lord was not in the earthquake. After the earthquake there was a fire, but the Lord was not in the fire. After the fire there was a tiny, whispering sound. When Elijah heard this, he hid his face in his cloak and went and stood at the entrance of the cave. He seemed to know that the Lord could be found in this tiny, whispering sound.

Take the time to listen to that soft and gentle voice. *Remember, the Holy Spirit's voice is only as loud as our willingness to listen.*

Chapter 13

The Power of Prayer

Throughout this life, we tend to take on many different personas. We are players on the grand stage of life and our roles are constantly changing. Certain situations require us to act in certain ways and many times we lose ourselves in the character we are trying to portray. In every role, from the corporate businessperson to the supermom, we change our mannerisms to fit the need. We want to appear in control, unafraid, determined and powerful. We change the way we dress because we want to seem "professional." We even change the way we speak, to appear more "businesslike."

After a while we begin to believe the image we try to portray, that we are capable of controlling everything and everyone around us. And this misconception can be extremely harmful to us, until we recognize it for what it is, an illusion.

Through prayer, we dispel the illusion. When you pray to that higher power, you acknowledge the fact that there is something greater than yourself and that you can't do it all. Your heavenly Father knows you as you truly are. It is pointless to try to portray another character to Him. He knows the real you.

You may be able to fool others, and many times even yourself, but you'll never be able to fool Him. He knows your gifts, your strengths, your joys and your achievements. But He also knows every fault, every hurt, every weakness and every failing. He even knows every secret thought and desire. Things that remain hidden from others lie unveiled before Him. Thoughts and feelings that, if known, would make others run from you, lie bare before Him. But instead of being vulnerable in this humble state, you have strength beyond measure—all because of one simple fact: He loves you. He sees you as you truly are and He still loves you. Doesn't it boggle your mind that someone can know every single thing about you, even your deepest, darkest secrets, and still love you beyond anything you can imagine?

Prayer is faith in its simplest and purest form because in prayer you surrender yourself to that love.

But many times people don't know how to pray. They get lost in the ritual of it or in a monologue of words that have very little meaning to them. In the process, they lose that closeness with their Father. It places a distance between them because they can't relate; it's as if God is off there somewhere in the distance and they're here.

Prayer is not difficult. Just keep it simple. There's no need for formalities or putting on airs; remember, you're talking to the One who knows every corner of your heart and soul and still loves you. When you pray to Him, you are not the corporate executive or the supermom or the teacher or the doctor, you are His child. Surrender yourself to His love and simply speak from the heart. And through that simplicity of prayer, great miracles will occur.

I remember the story of a bishop who journeyed across the ocean to visit a church. At one point, the ship he was traveling on stopped at an island for provisions. As the bishop walked along the shore, he came upon three fishermen, sitting by the sea, mending their nets. He stopped to talk to them, and as he did so they began to ask him questions.

"Why you wear dress like dat?" they asked.

"This is not a dress. It is a bishop's robe," he replied.

"What is bishop?" they asked.

"It is a Christian leader."

The fishermen became excited. "We Christians!" they said proudly, as they pointed to one another.

The bishop was a little unsure and asked them if they knew the Lord's Prayer. They had never heard of it.

"Well, when you pray, what do you say?" the bishop asked.

"We pray, 'We are three, you are three, have mercy on us.'"

The bishop was aghast. "Oh no, that will not do," he said.

He sat down next to the fishermen and spent the rest of the day teaching them the Lord's Prayer. The poor fishermen were eager to learn, and before the boat sailed away, they could recite the entire prayer without any mistakes.

The bishop was proud of what he had done.

After his visit to the church, the bishop sailed for home again. As his ship neared the island, he recalled the three fishermen he had met on his previous visit and vowed to see them again. As he stood on the deck thinking, he noticed a light on the horizon near the island. It seemed to get closer and closer. As he stared at it, he realized it was the three fishermen, walking on the water toward the ship! The bishop stared in awe, and when the three fishermen were within speaking distance, one of them called out, "Bishop, we hurry, come meet you."

The shocked bishop asked, "What is it you want?"

"We so sorry. We forget beautiful prayer. We say, 'Our Father who are in heaven, hallowed be your name,' but den we forget and no remember. Please tell us again how to pray."

The bishop was humbled. "My friends, go back to your homes, and when you pray, simply say, 'We are three, You are three, have mercy on us.'"

I believe that some of the most powerful prayers are the simplest ones because these come from the heart. The simple prayer that I prayed, "Heavenly Father, hold me because I really need to be held right now," helped guide me in a powerful way. When I prayed those words, I had reached a low point. I felt lost and unsure about what to do. I wasn't trying to put in my own ideas, because I didn't have any left. I was humbled, and in that humble state I was open to receive the information and guidance I needed.

Have you ever tried to help children who came to you for guidance when they were upset about something? You try to give them advice, but they're too upset to listen to what you have to say. They may be too angry or hurt. They may feel confused and betrayed. And the more you try to talk to them, the more upset they become because "you just don't understand—you're no help at all!" It's only when they reach the point where they are open and willing to accept your help that you are able to give it.

It's the same with our Heavenly Father. Many times when we pray, we are not truly ready to accept His help. Instead of letting it go and placing it in His hands, we hold on to it and try to fix it ourselves because, after all, we should be able to do something about it.

Once you place it in His hands, there is nothing else you need to do. Surrender yourself to that perfect love, secure in the knowledge that He will answer your prayers. In Matthew 7:7-11, Jesus tells us, "Ask and it will be given to you; seek and you will find; knock and the door will be opened unto you. For everyone who asks, receives; and the one who seeks, finds; and to the one who knocks, the door will be opened. Which one of you would hand his son a stone when he asks for a loaf of bread, or a snake when he asks for a fish? If you then, who are imperfect, know how to give good gifts to your children, how much more will your heavenly Father give good things to those who ask him."

Even with such a beautiful promise we still have a tendency to hold on to problems. Have you ever prayed for help and placed your problem in God's hands, only to find yourself a little while later wondering what you could do about this problem? Maybe it's because your faith wasn't strong enough. Or maybe it's because you were still living under the delusion that you could control everything. Perhaps you just couldn't fathom the depth of such unconditional love. Whatever the reason, learn to recognize this tendency and overcome it. Whenever I find myself wondering what I can do, I immediately turn it around by saying, "Thank you, Lord, for doing it for me."

I have learned that simply saying "thank you" is a powerful prayer, and I use it often now throughout the day.

I first learned its importance a few years ago when I woke up one morning to find that I was passing blood. My wife insisted that I go to the doctor but I hesitated, telling her that it was probably nothing serious and it would most likely

211

stop soon. That was not the case, however, and as the morning passed, it got progressively worse. I had appointments that afternoon, so I asked my wife to call and reschedule them and then meet me at the hospital when she was through.

At the emergency room, they attended to me right away. The doctor began examining me but couldn't figure out what was causing the bleeding. The nurses tried to begin an IV but were unable to do so because my veins were collapsing. The doctor said that he would have to make an incision to get the IV going and that I might even need a transfusion.

Already weak from loss of blood and seeing how frantically they were working, I became frightened. I began to think that this could be it. I could die right here in this emergency room. I couldn't say good-bye to my wife or children or tell them one more time how much I loved them.

I began to think of things I wish I had done when suddenly it became difficult to see. I began to experience tunnel vision. I could no longer see anything on either side of me, only what was directly in front. I felt my insides begin to shake, and suddenly my whole body was shaking violently.

They were trying to hold me down to keep me from shaking, when the doctor came in and said that he would have to make that incision now. When he cut, he must have hit a nerve because my finger popped back and stung as if it were on fire.

I was beyond frightened now, and a tear began to roll down my cheek. I don't know why, but I focused my attention on that tear, and as it rolled down my cheek I said, "Thank you, Jesus. Thank you for bringing me to where I am today. Thank you for being with me when I was really down. Thank you for healing me and touching me. Thank you for the people you sent to me. Thank you for my wife, my family. Thank you for everything."

I hadn't realized it, but as I thanked him the shaking subsided. My vision had come back, and with it came a knowing that I was going to be all right. I was filled with peace.

When they rolled me out into the hallway, I saw my wife standing there crying. They wouldn't let her back to see me. I stopped them. "Hold on, wait a minute!" I turned to my wife and said, "Baby, don't cry, it's all right. I know I'm going to be all right."

After some X-rays, they found the source of the problem. I didn't realize it, but the bleeding had stopped sometime between receiving the "knowing" and intensive care. I didn't require a transfusion and only spent one night in the hospital.

About a week later, I had a minor corrective procedure and have never had another problem. Once again, God had touched me in a powerful way, and I was left with a feeling that there was something I needed to learn from this experience.

I felt if perhaps I could go off alone for a little bit, maybe on a retreat, the answer might come to me.

I called a friend of mine who had about thirty acres of property in the country, some of which was designed as a meditation garden, and asked if I could go there. He said that wouldn't be a problem at all and I could go whenever I wanted.

I set out early one morning. It was beautiful, with plenty of woods and secluded meditation areas. I was all alone and spent the day quietly praying and meditating. I read scriptures and other inspirational material. I wandered the paths and reveled in God's beauty. I even quietly lay on an old, rugged cross that was there. But no answers came to me.

I left later that evening, feeling disappointed. Although it had been a beautiful day, I had hoped to discover what God wanted me to learn from my experience in the hospital.

Feeling somewhat discouraged, I headed home. I had planned on going to a meeting that night of the National Society of Clinical Hypnotherapists, but I just didn't feel like going anymore. I was disappointed and felt that there would be no point in going.

I was on the interstate close to home, and for some unknown reason I took the next exit and turned around. I decided to go to the meeting even though I knew that at this point I would be late.

When I arrived, the meeting had already started, so I excused myself and sat down. There was only one empty chair. I didn't want to interrupt by asking what they were going to discuss, so I picked up a book on the floor next to me. As I did so, however, I noticed a piece of paper on the floor, underneath the book. It was a photocopy and I didn't know where it had come from, but this is what it read:

Be not afraid. I am your God, your Deliverer. From all evil, I will deliver you. Trust me. Fear not.

Never forget your "Thank you." Do you not see it is a lesson? You must say "Thank you" on the grayest days. You must do it. All cannot be light unless you do. This is a gray-day practice. It is absolutely necessary.

My death upon the Cross was not only necessary to save the world, it was necessary if only to train My disciples. It was all a part of their training: My entering Jerusalem in triumph; My washing the disciples' feet; My sorrowful time in Gethsemane; My being despised, judged, crucified, buried. Every step was necessary to their development—and so it is with you.

If a gray day is not one of thankfulness, the lesson has to be repeated until it is. Not to everyone is it so. But only to those who ask to serve Me well, and to do much for Me.

A great work requires a great and careful training.

In my heart, I knew this was what I needed to learn: to be thankful for all things, even in the tough times, because it is through them that we grow spiritually.

When you pray, you must pray with faith, faith that your heavenly Father will hear your prayers and answer them. I find that thanking God first, strengthens faith. It's much the same as if you asked a friend to give you a ride home and he tells you, "Sure, no problem." The first thing you do is thank him. Now, you haven't received your ride home yet, but you still thank him. Why? Because you have faith in him that he will keep his promise. Would God do any less? Remember, "Ask and you shall receive, seek and you shall find, knock and the door shall be opened unto you."

So the next time you pray, remember to thank Him first, even before He answers your prayers.

Unfortunately, many times we fall into the trap of being discouraged or upset with God because we feel He didn't answer our prayers. Know this: God always answers prayers.

Just because your prayers weren't answered in the way you wanted them to be answered, doesn't mean that you were not spiritual enough. It doesn't mean that you didn't pray hard enough. It doesn't mean that you didn't say the right words, and it doesn't even mean that you lacked faith. He may not answer them exactly the way *we* want them answered. But you must remember, we are only human and we pray from a limited viewpoint. He is almighty and He sees a greater vision. And as with any loving parent, He may not give you what you *want*, but I guarantee He will give you what you *need*.

A few years ago a woman made an appointment with me for her six-year-old little boy. His fear of the dark had become so pronounced that he wouldn't sleep alone, wouldn't walk into a dark bathroom and was afraid of the "bad guys in his closet."

During the session, I told him that he had a guardian angel that would protect and help him and I asked him to visualize what his angel looked like.

The session went well and two weeks later I received this letter from his mother:

Dear Louie,

I'm sorry that I am so late writing this note to you. I wanted to tell you about the progress Beau has made since we visited you. The first day was incredible. Beau entered the dark bathroom all alone and even spoke of sleeping in his own bed, but as bedtime approached, he relented and slept with us as usual. Within a few days we were back escorting him to the bathroom again.

I questioned Beau about his guardian angel and he told us "she's on vacation." I pressed him a little harder and he tells us that his angel can't fight off what it is he fears the most.

However, all is not lost. His angel may not be strong enough to fight those foes in the closet, but she apparently has skills far greater than I and most of the doctors we've seen. An asthma attack stopped right after it began, with the aid of his guardian angel.

In his short 6 years of asthma, categorized as a 10 by our insurance company, an attack has never just quit before it could run its full course. Beau fell asleep in my arms as we called on his angel to help him. Within an hour, the attack stopped. His own response was "My guardian angel did it, Mom. She just slipped inside of me and the next thing I know, I'm breathing again."

As stupid as this may sound, I'll take the foes in the closet before an asthma attack any day! So it appears Beau failed to benefit too much from our session, but in some ways, the results were far better than expected. If only one asthma attack is prevented, that's progress as far as I'm concerned. I can't wait to tell his pediatrician.

With my most sincerest heart, I thank you for everything you did for Beau. I pray daily that his guardian angel remembers the secret to preventing an asthma attack. And for the time being, I'll fight the foes in the closet. It's the least I can do!

Thanks again, Louie,

Pam

Maybe Beau's angel couldn't fight his fear of the dark because it was *his* fear and he had to learn to let it go himself. His angel couldn't do it for him. Or perhaps he kept his fear in order to keep the comfort and security of knowing that his parents were always there for him. Whatever the reason, his mother didn't receive the results she came looking for, but God did give them what they needed.

I am reminded of the story of a preacher who was approached by a couple in his congregation. They had been trying to have a child for a few years but were unable to do so. They asked the preacher to please pray for them and he agreed, reminding them to have faith that the Lord would answer their prayers.

A few months later, they excitedly told the preacher that they were expecting a child and asked him to pray with them that their child would be born perfect.

For nine months, they prayed for a perfect child, but when their daughter was born, they were heartbroken to discover that she had Down's Syndrome.

"Why?" they questioned. "Why would God do this to us? We waited so long for a child and we prayed for it to be perfect. Why would He give us an abnormal child?"

The preacher felt bad but was unable to give them an answer.

The couple left the congregation and moved out of town.

Eighteen years passed, and one day the preacher saw the family again in a local store. "We have truly been blessed by our daughter, Mary," they told him. "She has changed our lives for the better. We do a lot of charity work now, helping other families and children, and we are truly happy. Mary has taught us the meaning of unconditional love. Before she came into our lives, we had never experienced that. And she doesn't know sin. She is so innocent and loving that every time we look at her, we see a glimpse of heaven. Our prayers were answered. We prayed for a perfect child and that is what she is, perfect."

What at first seemed to be a punishment from God was actually a blessing. This child opened her parents' eyes to another kind of life, one filled with love and joy in helping others, and one they would probably never have discovered had she been born "normal."

It's natural to sometimes question, "Why?" It's human nature. When something terrible happens, we feel we could handle it if only we could understand the reason behind it. But we must face the fact that we may not always be given that wisdom.

It's hard for us to understand and accept the death of someone we love, but especially so when they suffer a lengthy illness. Why would God allow them to die after we prayed so hard for them to be healed? Why did they have to suffer?

A few years ago, I stopped at a local print shop to have some work done. The owner, Forrester, was a casual friend, and in the course of conversation I asked him how he was doing. "Well, Louie, I'm not doing too good. I found out that I have prostate cancer and it doesn't look good. The doctors have only given me a few months, so I've been trying to get things in order. You know, with the business, the car—things like that."

I told him how sorry I was and that I would keep him in my prayers.

About a week later I was driving on the interstate, headed into New Orleans, when suddenly the thought came to me that I needed to go and see him. I decided that I would go see him later, but the thought persisted and became stronger: "*Go see him now.*"

Though I was about to cross a bridge and there was no turnaround, I did a U-turn in the median and headed back.

When I walked in, Forrester smiled and said, "I hope you're not here to pick up your printing order, because it's not quite finished."

"No, I'm not here about that. I honestly don't know why I'm here. I just felt I *had* to come and see you. Can we talk for a minute?"

"Sure," he said, "come on back to my office."

We went into his office and he sat behind his desk. I sat on a couch across from him and proceeded to tell him about what I experienced on my drive into town. I shared with him the story of my own healing and I told him that God can heal us at any time. He has a plan for each of us, and we just have to leave it in His hands. He shared some things with me, and we talked about all kinds of things, and before we knew it, a minute had turned into an hour and a half!

He got up from his chair and stood there for a moment. "Louie," he said, "I feel so much better about things, you just can't imagine. I really feel different. I needed this."

I felt such compassion for him at that moment that I stood up, put my arms around him and hugged him. "You know, Forrester, it's going to be okay. You're going to do just fine." And as I stood there, with my arms around him, I quietly prayed and asked God to touch him and heal him in a special way.

His wife later told me that after I left, she went into his office and found him crying. He said, "You know, Louie came at the right time. I needed this."

A couple of weeks passed and I thought about going to see him again to ask how he was doing, but the thought came to me, *"No, you did what I wanted you to do. Let it go."*

Some time had passed, when I received a call from him on Thanksgiving morning. He said, "I just wanted to call and tell you I received some good results from some tests. I just have a good feeling about everything."

When I hung up the phone, I felt that he would be healed. There was such excitement in his voice and he had a great outlook about everything.

About a year later, I saw his wife and asked how everything was. "Well, Louie, Forrester passed away."

I was shocked. This wasn't the outcome I had expected.

His wife continued, "But you know, those last few months he was so different. Even though the cancer was throughout his body, he was at peace with everything. He had accepted it and he even refused chemotherapy. He didn't want to go through all that. He died very peacefully at home." She even told me that right before he died, he saw the Blessed Mother by his bedside. He then took a few soft breaths and gently crossed over.

I had prayed that Forrester would receive a physical healing. God gave him, instead, a spiritual healing, one that made his crossing over easier. And Forrester, through his example of peace and acceptance, gave us something also. He showed us the peace that can come when we have that child-like faith. Through his dying, he taught the rest of us how to live. Yes, God always answers prayers.

Sometimes we may get the feeling that life has dealt us too hard a blow, that our cross is just too heavy to carry. At times like these we need to step back and realize that things could always be worse. I am reminded of the story of a man who felt overwhelmed by the adversity in his life.

He prayed that the Lord would take this heavy cross from him because it was too much for him to bear. Suddenly the Lord appeared to him and said, "I have heard your prayers and decided to take your cross from you. But you must know that in this life we each have a cross to bear, so even though I take this one from you, there will be another that you must take up. But I will give you the choice as to which one you will carry."

The Lord took him into a room and in it were crosses of every shape and size. There were massive crosses constructed of heavy timbers. Some were overpowering, made of concrete and steel. And off in the corner stood a small cross, hardly noticeable among the rest. It was tiny in comparison and appeared to be constructed of twigs. "I will carry that one," the man stated. The Lord smiled and said, "My child, that is the cross you asked me to take back."

There are times when our troubles seem too over-whelming. We can't understand why *we* were given such a hardship to bear. It's at times like these that we need to step back and take a look around us. Death, pain and adversity are all a part of life. God does not leave us to bear these things alone.

He gives us what we need to help us carry the crosses that come up in our lives.

One of the hardest things for anyone to understand is the death of a child. A few years ago, a client came to me because she was experiencing anxiety and was unable to get over the death of her little boy. During her session, she said she saw a group of children. Each one was happy and holding a lighted candle except for one child, whose candle was not lit like the others. She felt drawn to this child, so she walked toward him and asked, "What's wrong? Why isn't your candle lit?" And the child turned to her and said, "Because my mother's tears keep putting it out." Suddenly she knew that it was *her* child and that she had to let him go. He was in a better place and her anxiety about him was stopping them both from moving forward. After the session, she was totally different and said she felt relieved and at peace.

In that quiet moment, God had given her what she needed. It wasn't in the form of an answer as to *why* it happened; rather, it came in the form of acceptance that it did happen, and peace in knowing that they were both going to be all right.

Sometimes when storms arise in our lives, God doesn't take the storm away but instead calms His child in the midst of it.

Not long after this session, I received a newsletter from a local hospital. It was a newsletter that I received every month, with notices of upcoming meetings and talks. In it I read an announcement for a meeting of a support group for bereaved parents. I had seen this announcement many times before, but suddenly, the thought came to me that I needed to go and speak at that particular meeting. I didn't have a clue as to what I would talk about, so I tried to brush it off and continue reading. But I couldn't get the thought out of my mind. Something kept telling me that I needed to do this, so I picked up the phone and called the number listed.

When I told the coordinator of my intentions, she stated that she'd like to have me speak, but wasn't sure I'd be interested because it was a very small group. "It doesn't matter if only one person shows up," I told her. "I just know I need to be there."

She accepted my offer to speak, and after I hung up, I tried to think of what I would talk about. As my wife and I had also lost a son when he was only two days old, I knew I understood how these other parents felt. But beyond that, I was at a loss as to what to say. I knew that they would ask me questions like why did God take their child, and what answer could I give them? I didn't understand it myself, so how could I explain it to them? What had I gotten myself into?

I went into my office and sat in the chair. In prayerful meditation, I asked God, "Why do some children die? Some die in the womb, even before they have a chance to live. Some live for only a couple of days, or weeks or months. And some, Lord, die after only a few short years. I don't understand it. Why do You allow this to happen?"

As I sat there meditating, it was as if I could see this picture unfolding before me. All these joyful little souls were there with God. And God said, "I need someone to go down to earth to fulfill a part of My divine plan. Who wants to go and do this for Me?" Every little hand was raised excitedly. There were joyous giggles all around, as each one said, "I'll go, Lord! I'll go!"

They didn't ask how long they would be there or about the circumstances. They didn't ask what type of parents they would have or what type of place they would be going to. They didn't even ask God, "What is Your divine plan?" It didn't matter. They were happy and excited to do this for God, simply because He asked.

Then God turned to *your* child, smiled and said, "I would like for *you* to go." That little soul was thrilled beyond measure to be chosen to help the Lord fulfill His plan.

That tiny soul may have lived for only a short time, maybe only in the womb, or for only a few days or years. But in that short glorious time, it accomplished its purpose and then returned to God, the source from which it came. And that soul would see God face to face, for it returned as pure as it came.

Some souls will fulfill their purpose in a short time, while others will take a lifetime.

I feel that we who have lost a child at a young age have not really lost a child. We helped create an angel.

That talk for the bereaved parents, though they were few in number, was dynamic—not only because it helped those other parents release some of their grief, but also because it was a revelation to me.

As parents, we tend to think of these little souls as "my" child, "my" son, "my" daughter. But they are never really *ours*. They are His, first and foremost, chosen by Him, each with their own purpose, their own mission. These little souls are entrusted to us so that they might learn from us and we in turn might learn from them.

Through prayer I was given this understanding, and through personal experience I've learned the awesome power of prayer. But there seem to be many people who don't understand prayer and many others who are skeptical of it. Those who seem to need "proof" of the effects of prayer should be interested in research that correlates prayer with positive, healing effects on the body.

One such study was reported in 1988 by Dr. Randolph Byrd, M.D. In this study, 393 heart patients, admitted to the coronary care unit at San Francisco General Hospital during a ten-month period, were randomly divided into two groups.

He then contacted intercessory prayer groups and asked them to pray for one group of 192 patients. Every patient had three to seven people praying for them, but the patients were not told so by the researchers. These prayer groups did not pray for the second group of 201 patients.

The results of the study showed that the patients who were prayed for had significantly fewer instances of complication. They were five times less likely to require antibiotics to fight infections, and four times less likely to develop pneumonia; they had fewer cases of congestive heart failure, and none of them required life support from a ventilator, whereas twelve patients from the other group did require life support.

Another interesting study was reported in 1998 by Dr. Elisabeth Targ and her colleagues at California Pacific Medical Center in San Francisco. This was a controlled, "double-blind" study on the effects of prayer, or "distant healing," on patients with advanced AIDS. Those patients receiving prayer survived in greater numbers, got sick less often and recovered faster than those not receiving prayer.

It is also interesting to note that in December 1997, a study conducted by Beth Israel Deaconess Medical Center and Harvard Medical School found that 94 percent of health maintenance organization (HMO) executives believe that personal prayer, meditation or other spiritual practices can not only aid in medical treatment but also speed up the healing process.

There is a growing trend toward incorporating spirituality into medicine. I was excited to see that in my granddaughter Mandy's recent nursing textbook, *Nursing Now*, there is a section on spirituality practices in health and illness.

Some studies have even been conducted on nonhuman subjects, such as bacteria, seeds and wounded mice. These studies showed that the bacteria that was prayed for tended to grow faster, the seeds prayed for tended to germinate quicker and the wounded mice prayed for tended to heal faster. These studies are especially impressive because they eliminate the effects of suggestion and positive thinking, which in turn eliminates the placebo effect.

Still, many are skeptical about the benefits of prayer, and most probably they always will be. Trying to "prove" the power of prayer is like trying to prove the existence of God! It's not something that can be seen or measured, so skeptics will always find just enough room for doubt. It's like the old saying, "For those who believe, no explanation is necessary. For those who don't believe, no explanation is possible."

I am not a medical doctor, nor have I ever claimed to be. I can only share with you the profound healings that I have not only experienced myself, but also seen take place in others through the power of prayer.

In my private hypnotherapy practice, I have seen tremendous results take place by incorporating a person's spirituality in the therapy process. I have been approached numerous times by colleagues inquiring about the enormous success rate I've experienced with clients. The major difference between their approach and mine is that I incorporate a person's own spirituality in the therapy. Unfortunately, it is the one difference that some professionals have difficulty accepting.

One professional who understands the importance of working with a person's spirituality is Dr. Larry Dossey, M.D., lecturer and author of several books about spirituality and medicine. He tells of a survey conducted on the East Coast that found that 75 percent of hospitalized patients believed their doctor should be concerned about their spiritual welfare, and 50 percent wanted their physician to pray not only for them, but with them. According to Dr. Dossey, "Modern medicine is one of the most spiritually malnourished professions that has ever existed."

Dr. Dossey, in his book *Reinventing Medicine*, discusses the changing face of medicine as it relates to the growing trend toward spirituality. He describes three stages, which he refers to as Eras I, II and III, in the progression of medicine from the second half of the nineteenth century to the present:

Era I, which can be called "mechanical medicine" and which began roughly in the 1860s, reflects the prevailing view that health and illness are totally physical in nature, and thus all therapies should be physical ones, such as surgical procedures or drugs. In Era I, the mind or consciousness is essentially equated with the functioning of the brain.

Era II began to take shape in the period following World War II. Physicians began to realize, based on scientific evidence, that disease has a "psychosomatic" aspect: that emotions and feelings can influence the body's functions. Psychological stress, for example, can contribute to high blood pressure, heart attacks, and ulcers. This was a radical advance over Era I.

The recently developing Era III goes even further by proposing that consciousness is not confined to one's individual body. Non local mind—mind that is boundless and unlimited—is the hallmark of Era III. An individual's mind may affect not just his or her body, but the body of another person at a distance, even when that distant individual is unaware of the effort. You can think of Era II as illustrating the personal effects of consciousness and Era III as illustrating the transpersonal effects of the mind.

It's important to remember that these eras are not mutually exclusive; rather they coexist, overlap, and are used together, as when drugs are used with psychotherapy, and surgery is used with prayer.

I agree with his theories and I have seen instances in my own private practice that correlate with the concepts that are described in Era III. One such instance took place several years ago.

I had been working with a client, Kathy, who was experiencing severe stress and anxiety. We had approximately four sessions, and after each one she seemed to do better.

After an out-of-town stay, I returned home to find a message from her on my answering machine. Her voice sounded frightened as she said, "Dr. Bauer, please call me as soon as you can. I feel as though I'm having a terrible anxiety attack or heart attack, and they want to take me to the hospital. But I need to talk to you first." I returned her phone call that evening, even though it was past 11 p.m., because of the urgency of the message.

Her daughter answered and informed me that she was in the hospital. "We thought she was having a heart attack," she said, "but they found out it was a panic attack. Tomorrow they are going to run more tests, but she wants you to go see her in the hospital."

As I had been out of town, the next day's schedule was booked with client appointments and a prior commitment that would prevent me from going to the hospital that evening. I racked my brain trying to think of a way to squeeze in a trip to the hospital, but it was impossible to rearrange my schedule.

I decided to telephone her the next day. We talked for about twenty minutes and I explained that I would be unable to go to the hospital that day but I would definitely see her the following evening. She kept insisting, however, that she needed to see me as soon as possible. I could sense the urgency in her voice, so I told her, "Look, Kathy, as soon as I hang up the phone, I'm going to say a prayer for you and ask God to touch you and give you His peace. So, I'll be with you in spirit."

She agreed, and after I hung up the phone, I put my elbows on the desk, placed my head between my hands and began to pray. As I did so, an image popped into my head of a little old lady lying in a hospital bed. One of her legs was in some type of brace. It was raised in the air with ropes and pulleys that were suspended from a bar above the bed.

It was a sharp, detailed image that took me by surprise. I couldn't imagine why it popped into my head, and I found it difficult to concentrate on praying because my mind kept focusing on the image. The more I tried to pray, the stronger the image became. I just couldn't get it out of my mind. So, instead of focusing on the image, I decided to focus my thoughts on my prayer and just allow the image to remain.

Several minutes later, I finished praying and didn't think about the image again.

The following evening, my wife and I went to the hospital to visit Kathy, who was in a semi-private room. As soon as we walked in the door, I noticed the large metal arm and bracket that supported the television and suddenly remembered the image I had seen in my mind. My eyes immediately went to the woman in the next bed. She was elderly, but she wasn't the one in my image. Also, there was no brace on her leg and no metal pole above the bed.

Kathy was glad to see us and suggested we take a walk to the visiting room so we could talk. "I have to tell you something," she said. "As soon as I hung up the telephone yesterday, I remembered that you said you'd be with me in spirit and praying for me. And suddenly I felt better, much more at peace."

"Well, I have to be honest and tell you that I was having a hard time trying to pray at first," I said. "As I started praying, this image popped into my head." And I proceeded to tell her about it. As I did so, her facial expression changed. Her eyes grew wide and she said, "Dr. Bauer, when I talked to you on the phone yesterday, there was another lady in the bed next to me. It was an elderly lady and her leg *was* in a brace, raised up by one of those poles, just like you described! But she was in such pain that they moved her to a private room last night."

If we accept the fact that the mind or consciousness is not limited within one's own self, then we must also accept the fact that we are not just separate individuals, but on some level we are all united as one.

Dr. Dossey suggests that *"the non local mind is unlimited and boundless, which means that minds can't be walled off from each other. In some sense, at some level, we are each other."*

Isn't it possible then for us to be so in tune with that God consciousness, whether through prayer or meditation, that at times we have shared experiences, even from a distance? And could what I experienced be an example of this? I wholeheartedly believe so!

Remember, we are made up of mind, body and spirit. Mind and body are individual, different and unique unto each person. The spirit, however, not only completes us as individuals but also unites us as a whole, to each other. According to Ephesians 4:4-6, there is only one body, one spirit— that spirit of God which is in us, works through us and makes us one.

As I stated earlier, I believe that when we become more spiritual, we raise ourselves above the human level. Remember, I said "more spiritual," not "more religious." Spirituality goes way beyond that. Spirituality unites, whereas religion can divide. When we become more spiritual, we see things from a clearer, more knowledgeable point of view and are more in tune with God consciousness.

Some people refer to it as "collective consciousness," others as "universal consciousness." I refer to it as "God consciousness." The terminology really doesn't matter, and in fact can be another source of division. What does matter is that God is omnipresent—everywhere at the same time—and we, through Him, are connected as one.

Sri Ramakrishna, a Hindu mystic of the nineteenth century who spent his entire life trying to achieve true communion with God, preached a message of harmony of religions. He declared, "There are many paths, one goal." He studied and even practiced many of the world's religions, and came to the realization that all religions are the revelation of God, but in diverse aspects to satisfy the multitude of demands of the human mind. He believed that different religions were glimpses of one truth, but from different standpoints. They did not contradict but instead complemented one another.

It's like the old song: "The knee bone's connected to the shin bone, the shin bone's connected to the ankle bone," and so on. We are all members of one body, connected in one way or another.

Take as an example of this interconnection the events following the attack on the World Trade Center in New York City on September 11, 2001. The event didn't just affect those living in New York or even those in the United States. It affected people on a global scale. People around the world wept. They felt sadness, anger and loss. Everywhere, people felt traumatized. And everyone experienced a strong desire to help.

It didn't necessarily happen in their own backyard. It wasn't because they lost a loved one or friend in the attack. Why then this empathy and compassion? Traumatic events, such as this, seem to awaken something in each of us. They awaken the spirit in each of us that, in most cases, is repressed or held bound by everyday concerns that affect us as individuals. These events cause us to look beyond ourselves and the things we consider so important, and see them from a truer perspective. When people are filled with empathy and compassion for someone else, "self" ceases to exist and they become part of a greater consciousness.

It's the same empathy and compassion I feel when I work with clients. As I've said before, there is a time during each session that I pray for that person. It is not something done out loud, but it is something I am compelled to do. The prescriptions and affirmations I use during each session are predetermined on the basis of what the client is coming for. But many times during the session, I will change midstream because of something that comes to me. It's not an idea, in the sense that it's mine, but it's a thought or a feeling that compels me to act. And many times it requires me to step out of my comfort zone, because I might be embarrassed or unsure about how it will be perceived. Over the years, I've learned to just go with it, but it still requires taking a huge leap of faith.

One such case took place almost ten years ago. A woman, Georgette, came for a session to stop smoking. I conducted the session, and a couple of months later received a phone call from her. She was happy to say that she was still "smoke-free" and wanted to begin weight reduction sessions.

When she came to me for approximately her third session, she told me that she almost canceled her appointment for that day. I asked her what was wrong and she said that she was experiencing pain in her ear. A few weeks earlier, she had been informed by an ear, nose and throat specialist that there was blood behind her eardrum. He sent her for a CAT scan and told her that the only way to remove it was to cut the eardrum and insert a tube to drain the blood. She wasn't sure about this procedure and even went to see another doctor for a second opinion. He confirmed the first doctor's findings and agreed there was no other way to remove the blood. "As a matter of fact, I have a doctor's appointment scheduled for this afternoon," she said. "I'm going to get the results of the CAT scan."

We began the session for weight reduction and midway through the session the "thought" came to me: "*Place your hand over her ear.*" "Oh, I can't do that," I thought. "She's in an altered state. It might startle her." So I tried to ignore it and continue. But the thought continued: "*Place your hand over her ear.*" "How can I do this without it being awkward?" I wondered. But the feeling continued, even stronger, so I told her, "I'm going to place my hand over your ear now, and as I do so, it will help you to relax even more." As I said this, I gently moved my hand over her ear, careful not to touch her.

I began to pray for her, and as I did so, the "thought" said, "*Now put your finger in her ear.*" "No way!" I thought. "There is no way I can do that." I was afraid she would think it inappropriate of me to put my hand *by* her ear, much less *in* it! I tried to ignore it and continue praying, but the harder I tried to push it out, the stronger it became. "*Put your finger in her ear!*" "I just can't," I thought. "It's not professional. She might think I'm trying to do something funny."

She was peacefully unaware of the battle that was taking place within me. I couldn't even think of what to do next. Finally, I stopped myself and prayed. "Okay, Lord, I'm going to do this. I don't know why You want me to do this, but I'm trusting You that this is the right thing." As I quietly prayed with my hand over her ear, I gently placed one of my fingers inside her ear and continued praying. After a few moments, I sat down and finished the session.

As she was leaving, I blurted out, "The doctor is going to have some good news for you today." She smiled and said, "I hope so." After she left, I told my wife, "I don't know why I said that. I don't know what the doctor's going to tell her. I shouldn't have told her that."

The next morning, at 8:30 a.m., the phone rang. My wife answered and it was Georgette. "Deana, I just had to call you! You're not going to believe this—well, maybe you will! When I went for my doctor's appointment, he told me that the scan was good, there were no tumors in my ear and we could go ahead with the procedure. But when he looked in my ear, he pushed himself back in his chair and in a surprised voice asked, 'What did you do to your ear?' I said, 'What do you mean?' and he told me, 'It's gone. There's no blood in your ear.' He even pulled out a drawing of my ear that he had made on my last appointment and showed me that there was nowhere for the blood to go. He didn't understand it and he couldn't explain it, but my ear was perfectly healthy."

My wife excitedly handed me the phone and Georgette proceeded to tell me all about it. "You know," she said, "I hadn't thought about it before, but after that happened, it dawned on me that after my session my ear wasn't hurting anymore. The doctor just couldn't believe it. He had no idea where the blood went."

"That's all right," I said. "You know where it went, don't you?"

"Yes, yes I do," she replied.

It's not always easy to take that leap of faith. Sometimes it goes against every fiber of our being. We don't want to appear foolish, or we're afraid of what others might think. Sometimes we're intimidated by others and we place our own human limitations on His divine possibilities. But, I've learned that to see the miraculous, you're sometimes required to do the ridiculous.

I remember a particular client who had come to me because he was experiencing intense anger. He walked into the office and I immediately noticed his size. He was taller than me and muscularly built, but the thing that intimidated me most was the way he carried himself. His presence filled the room and I could practically feel the enormous chip on his shoulder.

I asked him to fill out a new client form and as I handed him a pencil, I accidentally dropped it. "Oh, I'm sorry," I said as I picked it up off the floor. Very aggressively, he said, "What do you have to be sorry for? You didn't do anything." Again, his mannerisms made me feel intimidated.

We sat and talked for a while and he told me how angry he'd been feeling, that he was at the point where he wanted to hurt himself or someone else.

We began the session and I brought him into an altered state. Near the end, at the point I would normally pray with a client, I thought to myself, "I'm going to have to let this one go. I'm not going to be able to put my hand over this guy's forehead and pray for him. He came in here so angry that if I try to put my hand over his forehead, he might take that as aggression and come up swinging.

When I had almost completed the session, I received the "thought," *"Put your hand out and pray for him."* "I don't think I can do that," I thought. "He was so full of rage when he came in and he's such a big guy, he could really hurt me if he took it wrong. He's just too big." And then the "thought" said, *"Yes, he is big—but I'm bigger. Just do it."*

I reached out and placed my hand over his forehead and prayed for him, and after the session, he was a changed man. He said he felt so much better and the anger and rage that had once consumed him was no longer there. He felt more at peace about the things in his life. He had come in like a lion but walked out like a lamb!

You can see how easy it is for us to put limitations on God. Just like a kink in a garden hose, doubt, fear and intimidation can restrict the inflow of God's healing grace.

We self-impose limits on what God can do when we pray with restrictions.

A client came to me one time because she was suffering with chronic pain due to arthritis. The pain made it difficult to do many of the things she enjoyed, like working in her garden. "You know," she said, "my children came down for a visit. It was the first time I got to see some of my grandchildren. And before they came, I prayed and asked God to let me feel better while they were here. I wanted to do things with them and I wanted to be able to play with my grandchildren. I told God that if I could just feel better while they were here, I'd put up with the pain the rest of the time. And I felt pretty good when they were here, but after they left, the pain came right back, even stronger than before."

"Don't you realize what you did?" I asked. "You placed a time limit on the pain. When you prayed, why didn't you just ask God to take the pain away and then let it go? Instead, you left room for it to come back in."

That's why it's important to be careful what you pray for. You just might get it!

The greatest results through prayer seem to take place when we're humble, when we seem to be at our weakest. At that point, there's no trying to put on airs, no trying to be someone you're not and no trying to handle it all by yourself. You're open, like a little child, ready to receive your Father's gifts.

That's where children have an advantage. They have not built up any preconceived ideas about what should and shouldn't be. So when they pray, it's with open and accepting hearts.

A few years ago, my daughter-in-law Ann called me and asked if I could work with my grandson Matthew. He had been to the doctor because of several warts on his hands. They embarrassed him, and although the doctor burned them off, they kept coming back. Ann was told by the doctor that the reason the warts kept coming back was because warts are caused by a virus and Matthew's body wasn't recognizing that virus as something foreign. I told her to bring him by and I would do a session with him.

When the session was over, I asked him, "Do you know what frankincense and myrrh is?"

"Yes," he answered. "It's the gifts that the wise men brought to the baby Jesus."

I said, "Someone gave me a special oil that contains frankincense and myrrh. Would it be okay with you if I put some on the warts and then prayed over them with you?"

"Sure, Grandpa," he replied.

I went to the cabinet and took the oil out. After placing a small drop on each wart, I placed his hands in mine and we prayed together, asking God to remove the warts.

Within a month, the warts were gone and he's never had another problem with them. He even told me, "You know, Grandpa, there was even one on my foot that you didn't know about and it's gone, too."

When Jesus said, "Unless you become like a little child, you will not enter into the kingdom of heaven," he didn't mean that we had to be a child. He meant that we have to have the heart of a child. A heart that doesn't doubt, a heart that sees no limits, a heart without restrictions and a heart capable of loving someone even after they've hurt us. Prayer from a heart such as this is mighty indeed!

But just like children, we sometimes keep trying to pound a square peg through a round hole. We keep pushing harder and harder, trying to do better, asking God to help us and then becoming frustrated because we don't see any improvements.

Don't beat yourself up. God does allow U-turns, and maybe, just maybe, He doesn't want you to do better. Maybe He wants you to do something different.

Chapter 14

Reflections

As I reflect on my own journey, I see things from a clearer perspective. I can now see how childhood experiences influenced my adult life.

I was born the only child of two very loving, but much older parents. As a young child, I was often teased by some of the children at school. It was your standard, hurtful, childhood fare but it sowed in me the seeds of anger, hurt and resentment.

This was probably the reason I became a staunch defender of the underdog. I could relate to them because I knew how it felt to be down. I developed a strong sense of justice, of what was fair and what wasn't. Without realizing it I was always on the edge, always watching and waiting for those instances of injustice because it wasn't right, it wasn't fair. It was these same feelings that later became the source of the depression I experienced.

These feelings and the resulting anger were always close to the surface. And because of this, the prayer I always prayed growing up was, "Lord, please teach me how to

241

love." As a young man and then a young father and eventually a grandfather, this prayer remained with me.

God always answers prayers. Looking back on it, I can see that everything I've gone through on this journey, experiences good and bad, the people I've traveled with and those He put in my path, were the stepping-stones I needed to help me reach the place where I am today. They were all necessary in teaching me how to love. Even what seemed to be the darkest moments, such as the depression, were vital in helping me to see the light.

I can now see that all along the journey, God was subtly trying to show me the way, but I was either too self-absorbed or too proud to realize it. And like the story of Saul in the Bible, sometimes God has to literally knock us off our high horse in order to teach us the lesson we need to learn. It was only after I was healed from the depression that I felt a more loving compassion for other people. Life was no longer just about *me*. God had touched me and helped me to see a bigger picture.

As a result of being able to see that bigger picture, the way I view certain situations has changed dramatically. I can honestly say that I no longer see the depression as a "dark moment" in my life. The anger, resentment and bitterness I felt were the dark moments. Darker still were the times I not only felt them but also nursed them.

At that time in my life I had never thought much about meditation. It was a vague concept, something Buddhist monks did high in the Himalayas. But the definition of "meditate" is "to ponder, to muse over, to contemplate or to mutter to oneself." In essence, then, it is a practice we all do every day during our entire waking hours. It's the self-talk we give to ourselves, and it can either be beneficial to us or destroy us.

Without realizing it, I was constantly meditating on the negative thoughts and feelings. By consistently dwelling on them, I gave them the power to totally consume my life. I created that fast-forward tape that ran within my mind, and once consumed by those negative feelings and emotions, I had no room for anything else. I had actually become my own worst enemy.

The depression was actually a blessing in disguise. There is an old saying, "When the student is ready, the teacher will appear." Prior to the depression, I wasn't ready to listen to that small, still voice of the Spirit. It took that traumatic event to "knock me off my horse" and force me to realize that there was something terribly wrong in my life.

Because I didn't realize the importance of forgiveness and letting things go, I held on to every hurt and injustice I experienced. I didn't notice it, because I just kept stuffing it down inside. Those feelings remained there, gradually building up over the years, until finally there wasn't any room left and I began to rip at the seams.

Once I allowed myself to forgive, I realized that I had been judging others according to *my* standards. I only saw the problems I experienced with my boss and my neighbor from one point of view—mine. "I would never treat someone like that, so how could they? I always tried to be considerate of others, so didn't I deserve the same respect? I try to do something good for someone else and it gets *me* in trouble."

This kind of thought process led to the "Me Syndrome." When you suffer from the "Me Syndrome," it's like living life with blinders on. It gives you a sort of tunnel vision where you can't see past the way things affect you personally. Forgiveness removes the blinders and allows us to see a broader view.

After that night in the chapel, I realized that my boss wasn't out to hurt *me*. He was trying to get the company through a tough time, doing what he thought would help the company build more business. He was doing *his* job.

I later learned that the "attitude problem" my neighbor had wasn't because he was out to get *me*. He and his wife were going through their own traumatic time with their children and with medical problems. The day he snapped at me, there were a lot more important things on his mind than my fence.

Forgiveness not only opened my eyes, it opened the door to love in my life. For where there is forgiveness, there is love.

Less than two years after my own healing, God taught me another lesson on the importance of love, and this lesson came through the death of my mother.

My father died when I was only sixteen years old, so my mother was all I had left. I feared losing her too. I loved her so much that I didn't think I could handle it when it came her time to go.

I was blessed to have her for many more years. When she was ninety-six years old, she suffered a bout of pneumonia. She remained in the hospital for two weeks but gradually got worse. The doctor came in one day and I was forced to face the inevitable. "Mr. Bauer," he said, "it doesn't look good. Her kidneys are not functioning properly. They're starting to shut down. There's plenty of fluid in her lungs and it's possible that she could drown in her own fluids. I doubt if she makes it through the night. If there's anything you have to do or plans you have to make, I suggest you do it now."

I was devastated! Even though she was old and unable to get around easily, her mind was still perfect. I didn't want to let go. How do you give up someone whom you love so dearly?

I called my daughter, Cathy, and my sons, Louie and John, and told them the situation.

They came to the hospital that afternoon and remained there all through the night and most of the following day. That night, my mother was in a semi-comatose state. She would open her eyes, come out of the coma a little bit and then return. Her breathing was labored and raspy from the fluid that was slowly building up in her lungs.

My heart ached as I sat by her side. I reached out to hold her hand. And in a motion that took me by surprise, she pushed it away. I reached out again, and again she pushed it away. She began moving her legs, as if she was uncomfortable. I didn't understand it and I didn't know what to do. What was wrong with her? And suddenly, the thought came, *"Ask her if she sees the light."* I couldn't do this. My mother was dying. How could I ask her something so ridiculous? But the thought persisted: *"Ask her if she sees the light."* I called my wife to my side, and said, "Deana, I have the strangest feeling that I need to ask Mom if she sees the light." "Then why don't you go ahead and ask her," she said. I felt so much better, as if I now had permission to do this awkward thing.

I turned back to my mother. "Mom, can you hear me?" In between labored breaths, she nodded. "Mom, do you see the light?" Again, she nodded. Suddenly I realized that her agitated movements meant that she was concerned about us. "Mom," I said, "your place is in the light now. Look, Mom, you did a great job of bringing me up and I appreciate everything you and Dad did for me and I love you very much. But your place is in the light now. It's okay for you to go there."

Her body movements seemed to calm down some.

My older son, Louie, came beside me and whispered, "Dad, ask her what she sees in the light." At first I was a little upset. My mom was dying. This wasn't the time to ask questions. But something told me that it was okay, that I needed to do this.

"Mom," I said, "do you still see the light?" Again she nodded. "What do you see in the light, Momma?" "Love," she whispered. She began to raise her hands in the air, as if trying to hold on to what she saw, and as she did so she took my hand and raised it with hers. "Love," she whispered again. "Louie, feel it. It's love." She continued to move her hands and mine, as if by doing so, she could make me part of what she was seeing and feeling. What a comforting feeling to know that the trauma we were witnessing—the labored, raspy breathing, the shutdown of her body—was something she wasn't consciously experiencing. She was somewhere else, experiencing something beautiful, and the only thing she seemed to feel was this immense love.

She made it through the night, and by the afternoon of the next day, there was no change in her condition. The kids had been at the hospital all that time, without sleep, so I told them to go home and get some rest and they could come back later. If there was any change, I would let them know. They agreed, and my wife and I remained with Mom. Although she never became fully conscious again, I spent the rest of the day by her side. Sometimes I talked to her, sometimes I just sat there gently stroking her hair.

Later that night, I told my wife to try to rest a little. There was a spare bed in the room that she could rest on and

I would sit with Mom. While my wife took a nap, I brushed Mom's hair and put some powder on her and just talked softly to her. It was close to 6 in the morning when Deana woke up and told me, "Please try to lie down for a little while." She was worried because I hadn't had any sleep. "I just can't sleep right now," I told her. "At least lie across the bed for a little while," she said. "You don't have to sleep; The rest alone will do you good. I'll be with Mom."

I lay down, and I distinctly remember saying, "God, I just can't go to sleep, hearing her breathe like this." Her breathing was so labored.

I must have dozed off because I don't remember anything after that. About an hour had passed when suddenly I jumped out of bed. I don't know what woke me up out of a sound sleep, but when I turned around, I saw my wife standing by Mom's side and she whispered to me, "She's taking her last breath." By the time I reached her bedside, she was no longer breathing.

Tears began to flow as I realized that this beautiful, loving woman was gone. As I stood at the foot of her bed, I looked out of the window. The sun was casting its first golden rays across the clear, unblemished sky. It was a beautiful morning. I turned back and looked at my mother's wrinkled, worn-out body lying on the bed, and it suddenly hit me, "She's free. She's finally free."

Immediately, I felt something all around me. I can't explain it, but it was as if I was enveloped in something. I turned to Deana and said, "I have the strangest feeling." And before I could say another word, she said, "You mean, like someone is hugging you?" I was taken aback that she knew exactly what I was talking about and I nodded. She smiled and said, "I feel it too!"

I was covered in a flood of emotion. My mother wasn't gone. Her spirit, her love were still with me. It wasn't just a nice thought to make me feel better. Her love was still there! It was something tangible, and my wife and I both felt it!

What happened next only confirms the tremendous power that love has in transcending all boundaries.

I told my wife, "We have to call the kids and tell them."

I looked at my watch and realized that my older son, Louie, was already on his daily forty-five-minute trek to work. As this was in the days before cell phones, I figured that I would have to wait until he reached work to let him know what had happened.

My younger son, John, had spent the night at my daughter's house, so I called her to let them know what had happened. When Cathy answered the phone, she started crying. "It's Grandma, isn't it?" I told her, "Yes, she just passed away." She and Mom had always been extremely close. Through tears, she told me they'd come right away.

As I hung up the phone, I decided to leave the room for a minute. I walked over to the door, pulled the handle and was shocked to see my son Louie standing on the other side of the door with his hand on the handle too. I was totally surprised. "Louie, what are you doing here? I wanted to call you, but I thought you were on your way to work. Son, Grandma just passed away."

Tears welled up in his eyes. "Daddy, I knew something happened. I was on my way to work and I was running late. Something told me to come here, but I knew I couldn't because I was already late for work. But something told me it didn't matter, I needed to be here. As I got closer to the interstate on-ramp, I thought I needed to turn and get on, but something told me, 'No, go straight.' It was like my mind and my heart were fighting each other. I just felt I had to be here."

I hugged him.

A few minutes later, Cathy and John arrived. Cathy was crying. "Daddy, I wanted to be with her when she died. I'm sorry I wasn't here. But right before I woke up, I had this really vivid dream about Grandma. I was in the hospital room with her. She was in the bed and I was sitting on the chair next to her, crying. And she was fussing at me because I was so upset. She said, 'Stop it, Cathy. I don't want you to do this.' I told her, 'But Grandma, I can't help it. I love you so much, I don't know what I'd do without you.' 'I love you, too,' she said, 'but it would hurt me if I knew you were doing this, so stop it, okay?' I told her I would try. And I noticed that the whole time we were talking, she was moving this little pink flashlight up and down under the covers. I could see this large circle of light coming through the covers, slowly moving up and down. And then Grandma said, 'Oh look, Cathy, it's going out. The light is going out.' And as she said this, the light under the covers began moving slower and growing dim. I told her, 'Don't worry, Grandma. I'll bring some batteries when I come.' Why I said this, I don't know because I was already sitting next to her. And then, it was as if someone was turning a dimmer switch. The whole room gradually got dimmer and dimmer, until the only thing I could see were her eyes. I immediately woke up and looked at the clock. It was 6:40. So I got up, started getting ready to come to the hospital, and then you called and told me about Grandma."

Were these merely coincidences? I don't think so. As I've said before, I believe that at some level, we are all connected—united through God, on a spiritual level, as one. I think that is why when my mother finally broke free of these earthly binds, we were still able to feel her love. It wasn't just felt by Deana and me there in the hospital room, but it was felt by my son on his way to work and by my daughter, a couple of miles away in her home.

You know the old saying "You can't take it with you"? Well, it's true. You *can't* take it with you. You can't take the nest egg you built up or the expensive toys you bought. You can't take the house, or the titles and degrees you earned. You can't take the money or the jewelry or the expensive car.

But there is *one* thing that you can take with you, and that is *love*. And love transcends all time and space.

God, the source of love, is eternal, which means love is eternal. Our physical death cannot stop something that existed long before our birth.

I received the answer I prayed for: God taught me how to love, or should I say He teaches me how to love? I've learned it's not a one-time lesson. Each day, through each situation and through each person He brings into my life, He continues the lesson.

It's not always easy to love, and sometimes I still experience that inner battle. That's part of being human.

In Matthew 5:43-48, Jesus said, "You have heard it said, 'You shall love your neighbor and hate your enemy.' But I say to you, love your enemies and pray for those who persecute you, that you may be children of your heavenly Father, for he makes the sun rise on the bad and the good and causes rain to fall on the just and the unjust. For if you love only those who love you, what recompense will you have? Do not the tax collectors do the same? And if you greet your brothers only, what is unusual about that? Do not the pagans do the same? So be perfect, just as your heavenly Father is perfect."

The difference between who I was before and who I am now, is that now I'm better equipped to fight the battle. I have my protective awareness shield, which helps me to recognize these situations and emotions for what they are. And I now know that the choice is mine: I can either overcome them or be overcome by them.

Keep remembering that the choice is yours and how you choose determines your quality of life.

Mother Teresa once said, "Don't think that love, to be true, has to be extraordinary. What is necessary is to continue to love. How does a lamp burn, if it is not by the continuous feeding of little drops of oil? When there is no oil, there is no light and the bridegroom will say: 'I do not know you.' Dear friends, what are our drops of oil in our lamps? They are the small things from everyday life: the joy, the generosity, the little good things, the humility and the patience, a simple thought for someone else, our way to be silent, to listen, to forgive, to speak and to act. Those are the real drops of oil that make our lamps burn vividly our whole life. Don't look for Jesus far away; He is not there. He is in you; take care of your lamp and you will see Him."

The more you practice love, the easier it becomes, until soon it will be as natural as breathing.

If we could reduce all of what God wants us to do into one thing, it would be love. That is the priority. However, according to Jesus, it is not one thing but three. We have to love God, our neighbor and ourselves.

We have to love God, the one who created us and loves us beyond measure. We can't stop loving Him simply because we feel He didn't answer our prayers or because life didn't work out the way we planned. It was never *our* plan. We are part of *His* plan. Our heartaches and problems arise when we fail to realize that. He is a loving Father who only wants good for us.

We have to love our neighbor. By neighbor, He doesn't just mean the person who lives next door, but also the bum on the street corner. Your neighbor is the person who bagged your groceries, the person who picked up your trash, the person who pulled in front of you in traffic and then flipped you off; it's the short-tempered receptionist, the jealous co-worker, the waiter who ignored you and the friend who talked about you. In essence your neighbor is everyone else in the world, the bad as well as the good.

And finally, you have to love yourself, whatever you perceive yourself to be. Many people have trouble loving themselves because they confuse it with being selfish or conceited. So they become harder on themselves. Self-love is really just self-acceptance. Learn to accept yourself for who you are. You are special, unique, "one of a kind," the original. Do the best you can with what God gave you. That's all He asks. It doesn't matter if you're an Olympic champion who finished the race first and won the gold medal or if you're a handicapped child who finished last. In God's eyes you will be rewarded equally. You don't have to be "the best." You just have to do your best.

Don't keep picking on yourself because you feel you don't live up to someone else's expectations. You don't need to measure up to anyone else's expectation of you. You're not on this earth for the purpose of being what someone else expects you to be. You don't owe it to any other person to be what he or she thinks you should be. Your main purpose is to

be what God created you to be, and in doing so, you will fulfill God's plan and purpose in your own special way.

Recognize your talents, as well as your faults. Then
build on your talents and work on overcoming the faults. And
let go of guilt and any feelings of inadequacy. They are a
hindrance to growth. Accept yourself. Love yourself.

A love that does not encompass all three of these—love
of God, neighbor and self—is incomplete. That is why I say
love is an ongoing lesson.

Life is fleeting, and in an instant it can all be gone.
Many of us rush through the day, consumed with a million
and one thoughts of "what I have to get done," and never
give a thought to how quickly it can all be over with.

If you were to find out that you only had one day left
to live, how do you think you would feel? I'm sure your
perspective on life would change drastically. Worrying about
the future would be pointless. Each moment would become
precious. And just about everything that had seemed to be so
important previously—getting ahead on the bills, achieving
more recognition with the company, choosing the perfect design and color scheme for the new house, saving up for that
vacation, and so on—would evaporate into an insignificant
mist, replaced by the things that are truly important: love,
forgiveness and compassion.

There's a television program that begins with the words
"Like sands through the hourglass, so are the days of our
lives." When that final moment comes, and our last grain of
sand slips through the hourglass, what is it going to be that
really matters?

When you are no longer here, how do you think others
will remember you? Better still, how would *you* like to be
remembered?

A few years ago, I had a dream that was so vivid and moving that I began writing it down as soon as I woke up. It touched me deeply then, and today I even use it as a prescription when working with clients, and have seen the tremendous impact it has had on their lives.

I'd like to share it with you in the prescription form, and as I do so, just imagine yourself in the story. You may find something beneficial in it to help you recognize the things that are important in your life.

Simply imagine yourself on a path leading up a grassy hill. It's a beautiful day. The sunshine is warm and you can feel a soft, gentle breeze.

As you walk along the path you notice the sky. It's a deep, rich blue, dotted with a few small, white, fluffy clouds.

In the distance, you notice an old cemetery nestled among the trees and you walk toward it. As you step out of the bright sun into the shade, you see an old wrought-iron gate leading into the cemetery. As you push the gate open, the rusty hinges creak with age and you step inside.

Everything is quiet. There's no sound except for the chirping of a bird and the breeze softly rustling the leaves, and suddenly you experience a feeling of total peace.

As you enjoy that feeling of peace, walking along the path, you come upon a headstone. On it is written the name of someone very dear to you.

(*Pause here for a moment and, in the privacy of your own mind, tell that person how much they mean to you.*)

Notice how good it feels to tell them that, and as you continue along the path, you keep that good feeling inside.

Off in the distance, you see another headstone. This one

is set apart from the others, and you can tell it has been left unattended, because the grass around it is overgrown. It seems like a very lonely spot, and when you stop in front of it, you realize that on it is written the name of someone who hurt you. Maybe it was something they said or did to you; maybe it was something they failed to do.

But here, surrounded by this wonderful peace, you can let go of whatever it was. You can let go of all the anger, hurt, fear, guilt or disappointment that you may have been holding on to. You can forgive this person and let it all go.

(Take this time and let go of those feelings. Haven't they controlled your way of life long enough? Right now, at this moment, be willing to let it go and turn it over to God. You no longer have to be a prisoner of those feelings.)

Once you make this choice, you will experience a deep inner peace and a joy unlike anything you have ever known. As you move on, you will feel lighter, freer and much better about yourself.

The path becomes much smoother now, and as you continue on, you realize how good it feels to be alive and free. You think of all your blessings and you realize and recognize all the talents God gave you, and you are thankful for the gifts and blessings you have.

(Pause now, take a few moments and become aware of the gifts and talents that God has given you.)

As you continue on, you notice another headstone up ahead. The sunlight is filtering down upon it and the grass around it is covered in wildflowers of every color and size. As you get closer, you realize that on the headstone is carved *your* name and underneath your name is a smooth space where nothing is written yet.

(*Pause here and take this time to think of what you would want written in this space, how you would want to be remembered by others.*)

Once that comes to you, hold on to it. Use it as your anchor. An anchor is something that holds you steadfast and stops you from drifting. So when you feel yourself losing focus, remember what it is that you wanted written on that space and reflect on it.

What I saw written on my headstone had a profound effect on my life. It helps keep me focused when I start to lose sight of what's truly important and helps me to see the bigger picture.

Just remember, it's never too late to change the course of your life. As long as there is breath in your body, there's time to change, a chance to improve.

Just because God healed me physically doesn't mean life is any easier for me. He didn't change the fact that I'm human and that I still experience the normal human emotions. What did change is the way I deal with them. Each time these feelings arise, I have to make a conscious decision not to let them affect me, but to let go of them. It's not always easy, but I do the best that I can and let go of the rest. I am truly a work in progress.

The journey is different for each of us and there are many paths to the same destination. There may be many things in this book that you don't agree with, and that's okay because this is *my* journey, and as I said in the beginning, just take what's yours, what can help you, and leave the rest.

Hopefully, through my experiences and the things I've learned, perhaps I can help someone else avoid the same pitfalls that almost destroyed me. If, through this book, I can help just one person to let go of past hurts, to change a negative perception or to experience inner peace, then I have done my best and succeeded in my goal.

I'll tell you now what I saw written on my own headstone: "*I did my best. Mission accomplished. Going home.*"

I wish you a happy journey, and remember,

What you are is God's gift to you;

What you become is your gift to God.

Afterword

I received this letter and poem some years ago from Dale Karen Cass, a woman who attended a spiritual retreat I conducted. She was a beautiful lady and enlightened soul who, I'm sorry to say, is no longer with us on this physical journey. But I wanted to share her poem with you because not only do I find it inspirational, but in her own words I feel she captured the true essence of the journey.

Dear Louie,

The retreat was very soul-cleansing and inspirational. You and Deana are truly special. You have given so much of yourselves to others and to me.

Enclosed is my way of saying, "Thanks." I have put my thoughts and messages from the retreat into poetic form; I hope you feel and enjoy the words as I do.

Love,
Dale

Meditation
Thoughts Taken from a Spiritual Retreat

Go within and find thee,
Let your free will take you there.
Explore the vast subconscious,
Be your healing strengths aware.

Cleanse your soul of anger,
Of fear and jealousy.
Happiness is a frame of mind,
Set the spirit free.
Own your thoughts and feelings,
Reflect—then let them go.
Be innocent of judgment,
From forgiveness peace will flow.

Just be still and listen,
Accept and reinforce.
Aspire to understanding,
Transcend a new life course.

Know that you are special,
In us a spark divine.
The altered state will guide you,
In the path of His design.

In this kingdom you are master,
Perceive and you will find.
The gift that God has given,
Lies unrealized in the mind.

—Dale Karen Cass

259

References

Chapter 1

Paul G. Durbin, *Kissing Frogs: The Practical Uses of Hypnotherapy*, Dubuque, Iowa: Kendall-Hunt Publishing, 1996.

Chapter 2

Geraldine Lux Flanagan, *Beginning Life*, New York: DK Publishing, 1996.

Thomas R. Verny and Pamela Weintraub, *Tomorrow's Baby: The Art and Science of Parenting from Conception through Infancy*, New York: Simon & Schuster, 2002.

Janet L. Hopson, "Fetal Psychology," *Psychology Today*, Sept.-Oct. 1998.

Internet site: www.birthpsychology.com

Internet site: www.healthhelper.com/complementary/book_mb/evidence.htm

Chapter 3

Internet site: www.epub.org.br/em/n09/ment/placebo1_i.htm

Internet site: www.healthhelper.com/complementary/
book_mb/evidence.htm

Bernie S. Siegel, M.D., *Love, Medicine and Miracles: Lessons Learned about Self-Healing from a Surgeon's Experience with Exceptional Patients*, New York: Harper & Row, 1986.

Bernie S. Siegel, M.D., *Peace, Love and Healing: Bodymind Communication and the Path to Self-Healing: An Exploration*, New York: Harper & Row, 1989.

Martin E. P. Seligman, "Optimism, Pessimism, and Mortality" (editorial), *Mayo Clinic Proceedings*, Feb. 2000, Vol. 75, No. 2, 133-134.

T. Maruta, R. C. Colligan, M. Malinchoc, K. P. Offord, "Optimists vs. Pessimists: Survival rate among medical patients over a 30-year period," *Mayo Clinic Proceedings*, Feb. 2000, Vol. 75, No. 2, 140-143.

Chapter 5

Paul G. Durbin, *Human Trinity Hypnotherapy*, Ann Arbor, Mich.: Access Publishing, 1993.

Sean F. Kelly and Reid J. Kelly, *Hypnosis: Understanding How It Can Work for You*, Reading, Mass.: Addison-Wesley, 1985.

Chapter 7

E. Arthur Winkler (some affirmations were presented at hypnosis classes at St. John's University).

Chapter 10

Internet site: www.pollingreport.com/religion.htm

Internet site: www.surgeongeneral.gov/library/
mentalhealth/home.html

Chapter 11

William H. Frey with Muriel Langseth, *Crying: The Mystery of Tears*, Minneapolis: Winston Press, 1985.

Chapter 13

Randolph C. Byrd, "Positive Therapeutic Effects of Intercessory Prayer in a Coronary Care Population," *Southern Medical Journal*, 1988, Vol. 81, No. 7, 826-829.

Fred Sicher, Elisabeth Targ, Dan Moore, and Helene S. Smith, "A Randomized Double-Blind Study of the Effects of Distant Healing in a Population with Advanced AIDS," *Western Journal of Medicine*, Dec. 1998, Vol. 169, No. 6, 356-363.

Joseph T. Catalano, *Nursing Now!: Today's Issues, Tomorrow's Trends,* Philadelphia: F. A. Davis Company, 2000.

Larry Dossey, M.D., *Healing Words: The Power of Prayer and the Practice of Medicine*, New York: HarperCollins, 1993.

Larry Dossey, M.D., *Reinventing Medicine: Beyond Mind-Body to a New Era of Healing,* San Francisco: Harper-San Francisco, 1999.

Chapter 14

Internet site: "Mother Teresa: Thoughts"
www.tisv.be/mt/thoug.htm

Dr. Bauer's Tapes and CDs

During the time that we are here on earth, we are going to experience some stress in our lives. Each day, we are faced with problems that we must solve in order to live a longer, healthier and more productive life.

Dr. Bauer has designed a dynamic series of cassette tapes and CDs. If you are experiencing a problem in your life, they will help you to overcome that problem in a calm, peaceful and loving way. The following topics are available:

- Deep Relaxation
- Stop Smoking
- Weight Reduction
- Affirmations for Weight Reduction
- Building Self-Confidence and Self-Esteem
- Overcoming Insomnia
- Preparing for Surgery
- Affirmations for Healing
- The Stress Buster—Overcoming Stress and Anxiety
- Freedom from Worry
- The Kingdom of God is Within You
- Be Still and Know That I Am God
- The Mind is a Terrible Thing to Waste
- Attitude of Gratitude—Be Thankful
- Blessing of the Children
- The Calming of a Storm
- The Rich Man
- The Passion

For more information, visit Dr. Bauer's website at
www.goodtapes.com